COMPUTER-AIDED TRANSLATION TECHNOLOGY:
A PRACTICAL INTRODUCTION

DIDACTICS OF TRANSLATION SERIES

Catering to the needs of students in schools of translation and interpretation, the textbooks published in this series are also very helpful to professional translators and interpreters who wish to improve their technique. The series' titles cover various fields in the discipline such as general translation and specialized translation as well as editing, writing, and lexicology for translators. Works that analyse the discipline from a more theoretical or practical point of view can be found in the "Perspectives on Translation" series. Both series welcome manuscripts written in either English or French.

In the same series

Jean Delisle, *La traduction raisonnée: Manuel d'initiation à la traduction professionnelle de l'anglais vers le français*, 1993
Jean Delisle, *La traduction raisonnée: Livre du maître*, 1993
Jean Delisle et Judith Woodsworth (dir.), *Les Traducteurs dans l'histoire*, 1995
Allison Beeby Lonsdale, *Teaching Translation from Spanish to English. Worlds beyond Words*, 1996

LYNNE BOWKER

Computer-Aided Translation Technology: A Practical Introduction

Didactics of Translation Series
University of Ottawa Press

© University of Ottawa Press, 2002

ISBN 0-7766-3016-4 (cloth)
ISBN 0-7766-0538-0 (paper)

Printed in Canada

Printed on acid-free paper

National Library of Canada Cataloguing in Publication Data

Bowker, Lynne, 1969–
  Computer-aided translation technology: a practical
  introduction

  (Didactics of translation series)
  Includes bibliographical references and index.
  ISBN 0-7766-3016-4 (bound) – ISBN 0-7766-0538-0 (pbk.)

  1. Machine translating.   2. Translating machines.   I. Title.
  II. Series

  P308.B69 2002   418'.02'0285   C2001-904318-X

University of Ottawa Press gratefully acknowledges the support extended
to its publishing program by the Canada Council, the Department of Cana-
dian Heritage, and the University of Ottawa.

This book has been published with the help of a grant from the University
of Ottawa Faculty of Arts.

Contents

List of tables

List of figures

Acknowledgments

I am grateful to many people for their support and encouragement during the production of this volume. In particular, my thanks are owed to Jean Delisle and Ingrid Meyer of the University of Ottawa, and to Dorothy Kenny, Jennifer Pearson, and Andrew Way of Dublin City University, who offered valuable feedback on earlier versions of this work. Any remaining errors or omissions are, of course, entirely my own.

I would also like to express my appreciation to my former translation technology students, in both Dublin and Ottawa, for their stimulating questions and discussions on many aspects of computer-aided translation technology.

Thanks are also due to the Faculty of Arts of the University of Ottawa for its support of this publication.

Finally, this project could not have been achieved without the support of my family – Keith, Joyce, Lisa, and Peter. This book is dedicated to them.

Abbreviations

This is a list of abbreviations used throughout this book. Appendix A contains a glossary that explains many key terms relating to translation technology.

ASCII	American Standard Code for Information Interchange
CAT	Computer-aided translation
CD-ROM	Compact disk read only memory
DBCS	Double-byte character set
EBMT	Example-based machine translation
HAMT	Human-assisted machine translation
HTML	HyperText Markup Language
ISO	International Organization for Standardization
KWIC	Key word in context
LISA	Localization Industry Standards Association
MAHT	Machine-assisted human translation
MARTIF	Machine Readable Terminology Interchange Format
MAT	Machine-assisted translation
MB	Megabyte(s)
MI	Mutual information
MIME	Multipurpose Internet Mail Extensions
MT	Machine translation
OCR	Optical character recognition
OSCAR	Open Standards for Container/Content Allowing Reuse
PDF	Portable document format
RAM	Random-access memory
RTF	Rich text format
TBX	Term Base eXchange

TM	Translation memory
TMS	Terminology-management system
TMX	Translation Memory eXchange
WWW	World Wide Web
XML	eXtensible Markup Language

COMPUTER-AIDED TRANSLATION TECHNOLOGY:
A PRACTICAL INTRODUCTION

0. Introduction

Technology is developing at a frightening pace and the demands made on the translator do not show any signs of abating. In fact, the translator is becoming more and more dependent on information technology and, if the translator does not adapt to change, he or she may become uncompetitive.

Samuelsson-Brown (1996, 280)

When translation and technology are mentioned in the same breath, many people's thoughts turn immediately to machine translation – the process whereby a computer program translates a text from one natural language into another. Machine translation has been around for more than fifty years, and the quality of machine-translation output has improved considerably over that time. There are apocryphal tales of early machine-translation systems that translated "hydraulic ram" into the French equivalent of "water goat" and "The spirit is willing, but the flesh is weak" into the Russian equivalent of "The vodka is good, but the steak is lousy." Machine-translation errors are not entirely a thing of the past, but they are certainly less common and considerably less outrageous than in previous times.

This is due to a combination of factors. First, advances in technology mean that it is possible to build larger databases of lexicons, grammar rules, and even extra-linguistic knowledge. Second, an improved understanding of linguistics means that relevant rules can be encoded more easily and controlled languages can be developed to reduce ambiguity. Third, better comprehension of the strengths of machines has led to new approaches to machine translation, such as statistical and example-based approaches. Finally, more reasonable expectations on the part of users mean that they no longer look to machines to be able to tackle any subject matter and produce fully automatic high-quality output. Instead, systems are being developed to operate in restricted domains that use a limited range of syntactic structures and vocabulary. In addition, pre- and post-editing are accepted as the norm, and some users are satisfied with output that simply allows them to get the gist of the source text (text that is understandable, even if it may not be publishable).

Nevertheless, when translations need to be disseminated to a wider audience, the quality of unedited machine-translation output is usually not acceptable. Although advances in machine translation continue to be made, for the foreseeable future at least, human translators will still have a large role to play in the production of translated texts.

This is not to say, however, that there is no role for technology in the translation process; in fact, quite the opposite is true. However, focus has shifted away from the notion that machines should be designed to replace human translators and is now firmly concentrated on the ways in which machines can support human translators. It has therefore become common to draw a distinction between human-assisted machine translation (HAMT), which is often shortened simply to machine translation (MT), and machine-assisted human translation (MAHT). MAHT is also known as machine-assisted (or -aided) translation (MAT), but these days it is most commonly referred to as computer-aided (or -assisted) translation (CAT).

The major distinction between MT and CAT lies with who is primarily responsible for the actual task of translation. In MT, the computer translates the text, though the machine output may later be edited by a human translator. In CAT, human translators are responsible for doing the translation, but they may make use of a variety of computerized tools to help them complete this task and increase their productivity. Therefore, whereas MT systems try to replace translators, CAT tools support translators by helping them to work more efficiently.

0.1 Aim

As Geoffrey Samuelsson-Brown noted in the epigraph for this introduction, technology is now an inescapable reality, as well as an absolute necessity, in the world of the translator. The aim of this book is therefore to provide a basic introduction to various types of CAT technology and tools that translators are likely to encounter and find helpful in the course of their work. In addition to describing the tools themselves, this book also addresses issues such as how translators interact with the tools and what impact the use of technology may have on the translator's working life.

0.2 Audience

This book is aimed primarily at translation students and trainers, but it will also be of interest to professional translators who would like to learn more about CAT technology. It assumes that readers have basic computer skills (e.g., word processing), and it therefore sets out to explain more specialized CAT technology. For the most part, translators are users, rather than developers, of technology. Therefore, this book does not attempt to explain the computational algorithms or technical implementation strategies used to build CAT tools. Such information belongs more to the domains of computer science and computational linguistics, and readers who are interested in delving into such subject matter might be better served by referring to works such as Trujillo (1999). Of course, the fact that translators are users does not mean that they have no role to play in the development of such tools. On the contrary, their feedback is invaluable for helping to guide improvements to the existing technology. Nevertheless, translators remain largely interested in the ends, rather than the means; in other words, they are interested in the capabilities that are offered by different tools, regardless of how these features are implemented.

0.3 Contents and coverage

The scope of this book lies firmly within the field of CAT. Limited discussions of MT will take place primarily as it relates to CAT, such as in the case of integrated CAT/MT systems. The decision to exclude lengthy discussions of MT in this book was made for two reasons. First, MT has already been the subject of much discussion and is particularly well documented in the literature. Readers interested in learning more about this subject can refer to works by Hutchins and Somers (1992), Bouillon and Clas (1993), Arnold et al. (1994), Melby (1995), Loffler-Laurian (1996), and Trujillo (1999) for enlightening discussions of both linguistic and computational issues in MT research and development, as well as detailed descriptions of different approaches to MT and of specific MT systems. In contrast, a number of the CAT tools described in this book have become widely commercially available only since the late 1990s, and they have not yet been extensively documented in translation textbooks (notable exceptions being L'Homme 1999a and Austermühl 2001). Also, as outlined above, the quality of existing MT systems has not yet reached the level where they can replace human translators in the vast majority of situations. However, CAT tools are increasing in popularity among professional translators. Therefore, translator trainees need information about the types of computer tools that they will encounter and be expected to use in the professional translation workplace.

In its broadest definition, CAT technology can be understood to include any type of computerized tool that translators use to help them do their job. This could encompass tools such as word processors, grammar checkers, e-mail, and the World Wide Web (WWW). While these are certainly valuable, possibly even indispensable, tools for a modern-day translator, they will not be treated within the scope of this book. Tools such as these are rapidly becoming part of our general knowledge. They are used by people in many professions, not just by translators. In addition, their use commonly extends beyond the professional world – word processors and e-mail are used for personal correspondence, the WWW is used to research hobbies, and so on. In short, most translation students will have encountered these tools in some capacity and will be familiar with many of their features. For students who are not familiar with them, a wealth of excellent literature is available, including some that is aimed specifically at translators. For instance, Haynes (1998) and L'Homme (1999a) describe techniques for using word processors and grammar checkers effectively in a translation context, while Bergeron and Larsson (1999) and Austermühl (2001) outline Internet search strategies for translators.

Some of the technology that is described in this book also reaches beyond the translation profession proper. For instance, optical character recognition (OCR) and voice-recognition technology can be used by anyone who wants to convert data into electronic form. Likewise, corpus-analysis tools are used by language professionals other than translators, including foreign-language teachers and lexicographers. However, these tools are not as widely available as word processors and the WWW, and they have not yet become part of the general repertoire of an average computer user, and so it is quite conceivable that translator trainees will not yet have encountered them. In addition, for some of the other CAT technologies described here, such as translation

Table 0.1   An overview of some different types of technology used in translation

HT	CAT	MT
• Word processors • Spelling and grammar checkers • Electronic resources (e.g., CD-ROMs) • Internet (e.g., WWW, e-mail)	• Data-capture tools • Corpus-analysis tools • Terminology-management systems • Translation memories • Localization and Web-page translation tools • Diagnostic tools	• Machine-translation systems

memories, term-extraction tools, and corpus-analysis tools, it is a prerequisite that data be available in machine-readable form. Therefore, it is useful for translators to learn how to convert data into electronic form so that they can then avail themselves of the more specialized CAT tools.

The other technologies described here are of interest primarily to translators. Some of these products, such as terminology-management systems, have been available for many years, but there have been a number of advances in this technology that will be discussed here. In contrast, other products, such as translation memories and bilingual concordancers, have existed in principle but not in practice. That is, the ideas were conceived of as early as the 1970s, yet it is only recently that such products have become commercially available. These tools are rapidly growing in popularity among professional translators, and consequently they must be included in the translator-training curriculum. Table 0.1 summarizes many of the different types of technology that are used along the continuum from human translation (HT) through to machine translation (MT). Most of the tools discussed in this book are best categorized as CAT tools; as such, they tend to lie toward the centre of this continuum and are shown in the centre column.

Of course, technology is not useful unless accompanied by instructions about how it can be applied. Translators must be trained in how to use technology to their best advantage and learn what types of technology will serve them best in different circumstances. Issues such as these will be addressed here, but it must be stressed that this book is not a user manual for any particular set of products. There are numerous competing products available for each of the types of technology described here. The specific workings of different programs will obviously vary – the user interfaces will be different, the programs may run on different operating systems or use different file formats. Nevertheless, these competing products are largely based on the same underlying principles. The purpose of this book is not to promote or to detail the features of any specific product (although a list of some commercially available tools is provided in Appendix B). Rather, the aim is to explain the underlying concepts and general issues associated with the technology as a whole. Once students are familiar with these fundamental concepts, translator trainers can follow up on the information provided here with tutorials or practical sessions that will allow their trainees to get hands-on experience using the specific products that are available at their own institutions.

Furthermore, for the purpose of clarity, and in an effort to make this book useful to a wide range of translators, this book examines technology independent of its application to any specific project. There are, of course, numerous examples used to illustrate specific points; however, this book does not provide a prescription for using technology to do legal translation as opposed to medical translation, for instance. Nor does it promote any particular approach to translation, such as the functional and interpretive approaches. What this book tries to do is to explain the basics of the technology. The application of this technology may differ slightly depending on the type of text or the subject matter that is being translated, or on the working languages or working style of an individual translator. For example, the specific search techniques employed when using a concordancer may differ depending on the language of the corpus, the subject matter of the translation, or the creativity of the translator. A wildcard search may be more productive in one language than in another, just as a context-sensitive search may produce better results in one subject field than in another. The parameters change from project to project, and it would be impractical to try to describe the minutiae of how technology can be used in every situation. Therefore, this book aims to describe the application of technology to translation at a more general level. It is only through experience with a particular product that translators can learn to take advantage of the features of that product, honing and refining techniques that can be used to get the best results in a given situation. Before this type of fine-tuning can be undertaken, translators must be familiar with the basic concepts, and that is what this book sets out to do.

Finally, there are a number of issues that, though important for users of technology, fall outside the realm of technology proper. For example, in order to use a concordancer, it is necessary to have a corpus. A corpus is a collection of texts in electronic form, but it is not simply a random collection of texts. The value of what comes out of a corpus depends very much on what texts are included in it, and special care must be taken to ensure that its contents are appropriate to the specific needs of the users at hand – needs that differ from project to project. Therefore, the issue of corpus design is a very important one, but it is somewhat independent of the technology used to exploit a corpus. In a similar vein, in order to compile a glossary using terminology-management software, a translator must first understand the principles of terminological research, and before using a translation memory to assist with a translation, the translator must first understand the principles of translation. These issues are clearly important prerequisites for making good use of technology, but they fall largely beyond the scope of this book. The main focus here is technology itself; therefore, issues such as corpus design and terminological and translation principles will be addressed only insofar as the technology itself has an effect on these issues (e.g., when the use of technology has brought about a change in practice). Otherwise, such topics will be dealt with only cursorily, and readers will be referred to works that focus more directly on these issues.

0.4 Outline

This book comprises six chapters. Chapter 1 addresses the question of why it is relevant and important for translators to learn about technology. This chapter looks beyond the simple answer of training students to use a tool in order to help them find jobs and explores some of the other benefits to be gained by including technology training in the translation curriculum.

The CAT tools described in this book can only process information that is in a specific electronic form, and chapter 2 explains how information can be converted into machine-readable form using OCR and voice-recognition software. It also addresses the issue of file formats, explaining how electronic data intended for use with one software application can be converted into a format that is suitable for use with another.

Chapter 3 explores the different features of corpus-analysis tools, including word-frequency lists, monolingual and bilingual concordancers, and collocation generators. The benefits and drawbacks of using these tools are outlined.

Terminology-management systems are the subject of chapter 4. Although this type of tool has existed since the 1970s and has been widely available to translators since the 1980s, there have been some recent developments, particularly with regard to increased flexibility of storage and retrieval, and these are described here.

Chapter 5 focuses on translation-memory systems – one of the newest and most exciting CAT tools to come onto the market in recent years. First proposed in the 1970s, this technology only became commercially available on a wide scale in the late 1990s, and it has been steadily increasing in popularity with translators since that time.

Chapter 6 looks to the future, briefly examining other new technologies and emerging trends that are beginning to be of interest to working translators, including software localization tools, diagnostic tools, new types of translation work, and the integration of translation into the document-production cycle.

The book ends with two appendices. Appendix A contains a glossary of important terms and concepts related to translation technology. Appendix B provides details about a variety of commercially available CAT tools; it also suggests a number of questions that potential users might consider asking vendors when attempting to evaluate whether or not a given tool will meet their needs.

1. Why Do Translators Need to Learn about Technology?

If we don't train for it, perhaps it will go away?

Haynes (1998, 135)

By integrating CAT tools into our teaching environment, we are not merely imparting the kind of practical skills that will get graduates jobs. We are also creating an environment in which basic and applied research can be carried out into a number of areas, including translation pedagogy, terminography, CAT tools evaluation, human-machine interaction, and text analysis and composition.

Kenny (1999, 78)

Following the initial disappointment at the lack of fully automatic high-quality machine-translation output, many translator-training institutes chose to minimize the teaching of technology in favour of other translation-related issues. As observed by Kingscott (1996, 297), this has still sometimes been the case even in recent times:

> I have detected a certain complacency among some teachers of translation. Because they have seen that despite 50 years of research and development the impact of automatic translation is still very small, they think that translation will continue, by and large, to be practiced in traditional ways for a long time yet.

Similarly, Haynes (1998, viii) notes that many professional translators, and their organizations, remain remarkably uninformed with regard to the progress made in translation technology. He goes on to observe that many are also largely unenthusiastic about it – with attitudes lying somewhere between skeptical and scathing – their very ignorance seeming to contribute to their fear that their jobs will be threatened by this technology.

Kingscott and Haynes both issue warnings that the pace of change is beginning to accelerate. They foresee a dramatic increase in the use of CAT tools and note that this increase will be needs-driven, rather than research-driven. The long-awaited global market is fast becoming a reality. While it was once feared that the English language would dominate the global marketplace, many companies are actually finding that failure to translate results in a loss of international sales. A clear example of this trend can be found in the software localization industry. The term "localization" refers to the process of customizing or adapting a product for a target language and culture. According to Brooks (2000, 43), in fiscal 1998, Microsoft's revenue from localized products exceeded US$5 billion. Similarly, Thibodeau (2000, 127) observes that American software companies often report international revenues exceeding 50 percent of total sales. Thibodeau goes on to state that a major reason for localizing software products is economic – a product that is barely making a profit in the domestic market can be a highly profitable venture overseas, often increasing a company's sales by at least 25 percent. All else being equal, a software product that is not localized is less likely to survive over the long run. In addition, a localized product can help to spread research and development funds over a wider base because a localized version can extend a product's life cycle. While a domestic market is declining, an international market may be emerging or still growing, and sales abroad can help to finance the next generation of products. Furthermore, most products can be more profitable overseas because these markets often support higher prices.

Therefore, in order to stay competitive and increase profits, companies in a variety of fields (e.g., software, hardware, e-commerce, camera equipment, telecommunications, automotive industry) are localizing their products and Web sites. This has resulted in an increase in the volume of translation, particularly technical translation. Sprung (2000, ix) notes that market watchers at Allied Business Intelligence estimated the worldwide market for localization and Web-site translation to be about US$11 billion in 1999, and they predict that it will grow to US$20 billion by 2004. The increase in volume has been accompanied by an increase in pressure on translators to work more quickly while maintaining high-quality output. Many companies now aim to launch a Web site or release a product and its accompanying documentation in many languages simultaneously (or at least within an acceptable period following the release of the original) – a practice known as simultaneous shipment, or "simship." This means that translators are encouraged to work faster in order to reduce the time-to-market of a global product. Formerly, translation was considered to be the last step in the production process; nowadays, translation often begins while a product is still under active development. Leaving the entire translation process until the product is finalized does not facilitate simship, and so this conventional approach to translation is being rejected as a viable means of operation.

From a company's point of view, localization results in higher translation costs and a slower time-to-market. In a local market, product documentation may be delivered in only one language, and the product can be put on the shelf as soon as it is ready. In the global market, product documentation is first written in one language and then translated into many others, and if simship is desired, the product cannot go onto the shelf until all the translations are complete. Every week of translation time that is saved could have a major impact on product sales. Therefore, more than ever, companies are looking for translators who can work cheaply and quickly, but still deliver high-quality work. One way in which translators are trying to achieve this balance is by turning to technology for assistance.

Schäler (1998, 155) notes that the translation profession must take steps to resolve the tension between its traditional professional value system and the new technologies if it wants to participate in some of the most interesting and lucrative areas of translation activity, such as localization. In Schäler's view, this entails making some radical changes to the professional mind-set of translators, as well as integrating translation technology courses into all translator-training programmes. Schäler feels that by the time they graduate, translation students must be aware of the wide variety of translation tools available and have had some exposure to a representative selection of these tools. In addition, they should have learned about the financial and operational implications of the introduction and use of translation tools in a traditional translation environment. This is echoed by Kingscott (1996, 295), who warns that unless technology-related issues are integrated into translator-training programmes, there is a real danger that the university teaching of translation may become so remote from practice that it will be marginalized and consequently be widely perceived as irrelevant to the translation task. The gap between technological advances and pedagogical practices must be closed.

Schäler and Kingscott are not the only ones who feel that technology deserves a more prominent place in the translation curriculum. In recent years, increasing emphasis has been placed on the need to further integrate technology-related training into translator-training programmes. Otman (1991), Scherf (1992), Clark (1994), Gouadec (1994), Wältermann (1994), DeCesaris (1996), de Schaetzen (1997), Haynes (1998), Kenny (1999), L'Homme (1999b), and Austermühl (2001), among others, have observed that familiarity with CAT technology is becoming a prerequisite for translators, and they have drawn attention to the fact that translator trainers need to concern themselves with the sorts of skills that new graduates need in order to meet the challenges and survive the competition of the twenty-first century. Some, such as Clark (1994, 308) and Gouadec (1994, 65), have even gone so far as to state that universities have an obligation to equip their students with such skills since these are in great demand in the translation marketplace.

The existence of such a demand is not in doubt. According to Kenny (1999, 79), experience has shown that graduates who are conversant with CAT technology are at a real advantage when it comes to working in highly technologized translation environments such as the software industry and the organizations of the European Union. This trend is also increasing in other sectors, such as the telecommunications and automotive sectors. As Brooks (2000, 57) points out, the creation of the printing press eliminated the job of the scribe, but it created a vastly larger market for books, and consequently there was a greater demand for authors, editors, and illustrators. By analogy, Brooks notes that the development of CAT tools has not reduced the need for language professionals. Rather, improvements in efficiency and reductions in translation costs brought about by the use of these tools has stimulated a demand for localized products and created jobs for translators who are skilled at using technology. In fact, according to Rode (2000, 13), a new type of career is beginning to emerge for people who specialize in managing translation technology.

The principal aim of this book, then, is to provide an introduction to some of the important technologies that are currently available for helping translators to do their job more efficiently. It should be noted, however, that while knowing how to use such tools constitutes a valuable practical skill for any translation graduate, the integration of translation technology into translator-training programmes can also pay off in other ways. As Kenny (1999, 78) notes, when trainers integrate CAT tools into the translation curriculum, they are not simply imparting the kind of practical skill that will help graduates to get jobs, they are also creating an environment in which basic and applied research can be carried out in a number of areas, including translation pedagogy, human-machine interaction, and the evaluation of technology. In addition, if the CAT tools that are integrated into translator-training programmes ultimately change the nature of the job – and Kenny (1999) presents evidence to support this idea – then trainers must be concerned not only with teaching students how to use the tools, but also with investigating how the tools can actually change the translator's task.

1.1 Translation technology in the classroom: Laying the foundation for new types of investigations

As noted in the introduction, the principal aim of this book is to provide a basic introduction to various types of technology that a translator is likely to encounter and find helpful. Nevertheless, it is worth exploring some of the additional benefits to be gained by introducing translation technology into the translator-training curriculum.

1.1.1 Exploring the impact of technology on translation pedagogy

Integrating technology into the translation curriculum can have an impact on the way in which translation itself is taught. For example, a number of changes in teaching have been brought about by the fact that data are available in electronic form. Technologies such as optical character recognition and voice recognition can be used to convert data into electronic form, which makes it easier to share resources, such as corpora and translations, among students as well as between students and trainers. In a similar vein, the possibility of networking has also increased the shareability of data (Gouadec 1994, 73; Wältermann 1994, 312). For example, some types of technology, such as terminology-management systems and translation memories, can be networked, which facilitates the sharing of glossaries or translations.

DeCesaris (1996, 264) notes how translation memories can be used as a self-learning resource to provide students with immediate access to models that they know are correct. She goes on to explain that while the idea of providing students with models is not new, the point is that students are often given a single model for specific translations, which perpetuates the view that there is only one correct translation for a given text. A translation memory with fuzzy matching capability (see section 5.1.2.3) can make it easy for trainers to provide more than one good model for a translation.

Scherf (1992, 157) explains that in his experience, the use of technology has led to an individualization of the teaching process. Students can work at their own pace, while trainers have the opportunity to watch them in the immediate translation process, to discuss on the spot alternative solutions to any translation problems that arise, and to give individually relevant advice without the need to adjust the explanations so that the average student in the course might benefit from them. Furthermore, it is still possible, at appropriate points, to have class-wide discussions and to make observations of a more general nature.

Ahrenberg and Merkel (1996, 185) and Kenny (1999, 77) observe that the use of tools such as translation memories forces students to contemplate issues such as text type and to consider the intra- and inter-textual features of text. Since certain texts are more suitable than others for use with different technologies, students must engage in textual analysis to determine whether it would be beneficial to translate a particular text with the help of a specific type of technology. For example, an investigation into what proportion of single texts and families of texts are made up of recurrent units can lead to discussions about the degree of suitability of a text for use with a translation-memory system (see section 5.4).

Finally, Scherf (1992, 155) identifies the possibility of enhancing the pedagogical value of CAT tools by introducing a module that would act as a kind of intelligent tutoring system in computer-supported translation classes.

1.1.2 Investigating human-machine interaction

By reflecting on the nature of machines and how they work, students can learn to adjust their expectations about what machines can and cannot do, and they can learn to adapt their own working practices to maximize the benefit to be gained from using CAT tools. For example, Kenny (1999, 77) observes that one benefit of using translation memories is that they make students reflect on the precise nature of electronic text. While observing her students, Kenny noticed that most source-text segmentation errors that they encountered when using the translation-memory system were caused by intrusive line and paragraph breaks that they did not initially consider to be a problem because they would not cause problems for humans reading a printout of the text. Similarly, students learn that when using a concordancer, the system will return examples that precisely match the pattern that a student requests, which is not necessarily the pattern that the student wished to retrieve (see section 3.4.5). As students use technology, they become more aware of the fact that the computers are not capable of applying intelligence or common sense to a task in the same way that humans would. Students learn that they have to make things easy for the computer through techniques such as proper text markup, controlled language, and carefully formulated queries.

Experience in interacting with machines may also result in suggestions for improvements to the technology and lead to changes in conventional practices (see sections 4.6.3 and 5.5.2).

1.1.3 Learning to evaluate technology

As students learn to use a particular tool, they should also be encouraged to evaluate that tool in terms of its potential for helping them to complete their task more efficiently. Evaluations can be conducted on a single tool, or comparisons can be made between several competing products. As Otman (1991, 19) and Gouadec (1994, 70) point out, such evaluations may result in suggestions for improvements to the technology (e.g., development of better user interfaces or more flexible storage choices).

In addition, given the range of technologies that are available, students can also learn to assess tools in the light of a particular task or project in order to determine which type of tool can best help them carry out that task (L'Homme 1999a, 343; Sager 1994, 194). This knowledge can, in turn, be used to develop automated diagnostic tools (see section 6.5).

1.1.4 Examining how tools can change conventional practices

In many professions, and indeed in our everyday lives, technology is called upon to assist us with the tasks that we need to perform. However, it has been observed that technology can sometimes change the very nature of the task that it was designed to facilitate. Ahrenberg and Merkel (1996, 187), Heyn (1998, 135), and Kenny (1999, 71) provide different examples of how CAT tools have affected the nature of translation-related tasks. For example, when recording information on term records, translators no longer record just the base form of the term. Instead, they record multiple forms of the term so that they can minimize editing by cutting and pasting the appropriate form directly into the target text (see section 4.6.3). Similarly, translators who use translation-memory systems tend to formulate their texts in such a way as to maximize their potential for reuse (see section 5.5.2).

Scherf (1992, 157) and Kenny (1999, 73) note that translator trainers are now in a position to observe students in the immediate translation process and see what approaches and solutions they come up with when faced with the kinds of choices that technology presents to them (e.g., how should they record their terminology). Kenny goes on to contend that the instructors who are providing training in the use of these tools should monitor and report on such decisions with a view to developing new guidelines that take into account the interaction with new technologies.

1.1.5 Producing data for empirical investigations

An additional benefit to be gained from introducing technology into the translation curriculum is that a by-product of the use of this technology is the gradual accumulation of data that can be used for other types of studies. For some time, translation theorists (e.g., Holmes 1988; Toury 1980) have been calling for a more empirical basis for their discipline. Electronic corpora and translation memories can provide large quantities of easily accessible data that can be used to study translation. Bilingual parallel corpora (such as those produced through alignment or by using translation-memory systems) can be used to investigate translation strategies and decisions. For instance, Ebeling (1998) has used a bidirectional parallel corpus of Norwegian and English texts to examine the behaviour of presentative English *there*-constructions as well as the equivalent Norwegian *det*-constructions in original and translated English and original and translated Norwegian, respectively. Similarly, Maia (1998) has used a bidirectional parallel corpus of English and Portuguese texts to analyze the nature and frequency of the subject-verb-object sentence structure in original and translated English and in original and translated Portuguese.

In addition to being used for research applications, the data generated can be used for pedagogical applications. For example, trainers can build an archive of student translations, which can be used to guide teaching practices. For example, the following types of corpora could be extracted from an archive of student translations.

First, a trainer can extract a text-specific corpus consisting of all translations of a given source text done by the students in a particular class. Using a corpus-analysis tool such as a concordancer, the trainer can then examine corresponding sections of all the translations simultaneously. This allows the trainer to identify areas where the class as a whole is having difficulty, as distinct from problems that may have befallen only one or two students. Spotting patterns of this type is much more difficult and cumbersome when working with separate sheets of paper.

Many translation courses are devoted to specialized subject fields, such as legal, medical, or economic translation. Trainers can extract a corpus of translations pertaining to a particular subject field and examine these to determine whether a problem is specific to a particular source text or is a difficulty that also manifests itself in other texts dealing with a related subject. For example, when translating a text in the subject field of law, students might have difficulty constructing the proper syntax because one particular source text is awkwardly worded and is negatively influencing their target-language production, or they may be having difficulty coming to grips with legal syntax in general.

Corpora that span multiple subject fields can be extracted to investigate, for instance, whether the problems encountered by a group of students in their French technical-translation course are similar to or different from the problems they are having in their French economic-translation course. A trainer can investigate whether a student is having a problem that results from a poor knowledge of grammar (and thus manifests itself regardless of the subject field) or having difficulty caused by a lack of knowledge of the vocabulary or syntax of a particular specialized language (a problem that is not in evidence when translating texts in a different subject field).

Cross-linguistic/same-subject-field corpora can also be extracted to examine the impact of source-language interference. For example, a student may be taking two different courses in economic translation: one from French and one from Spanish. A comparison of the two sets of translations may reveal that a student is having different types of problems when translating out of French than when translating out of Spanish, in which case it may be necessary to focus on source-language interference, or it may turn out that a student is having similar problems regardless of the source language (e.g., perhaps the student has not grasped the concept of "register"), in which case it may be necessary to tackle the issue in a non-source-language-related way.

Finally, longitudinal studies can be carried out to chart the progress of individual students or groups of students, and these can be performed over the course of a semester, a year, or even an entire degree. Using such a corpus, a trainer (or even a student) can see which problems appear to have been resolved and which are still causing difficulties.

Another type of longitudinal study could be conducted if a trainer decides to try a new teaching method from one year to the next. If the trainer has used the same source text (or even different texts that pose similar translation difficulties) with more than one group of students, it may be interesting for him or her to compare the translations done by a class who were taught using the "old" method with those of a class who were taught using the "new" method. While a comparison of this sort would not be enough to enable the trainer to make definitive claims about the usefulness of one teaching method over another, it may nevertheless reveal some interesting points worthy of further investigation.

1.1.6 Reinforcing basic translation skills

The examples discussed above provide an indication of new types of translation-related investigations that become possible through the use of technology. At the same time, however, it should be emphasized that time spent teaching technology does not necessarily take away from time spent on other translation skills. In fact, if technology is properly integrated into the translation classroom, it not only allows the students to develop new skills, it also leads to an intensification of the basic translation curriculum. As de Schaetzen (1997, 18) and L'Homme (1999b, 118) point out, students who use technology to produce term records, find solutions in parallel documentation, or produce actual translations are reinforcing these basic translation skills as well as developing good and realistic working practices that can later be applied in the workplace.

KEY POINTS

- The use of translation technology is on the rise, and this increase is needs-driven – the global market has resulted in a greater volume of translation along with increased pressure to produce translations quickly in order to facilitate simship.

- Familiarity with CAT technology is becoming a prerequisite for translation students if they are to be able to meet the challenges and survive the competition of the twenty-first century.
- In addition to being a valuable practical skill for any translation graduate, integration of translation technology into translator-training programmes can pay off in other ways, such as reinforcing basic translation skills, producing data that can be used for empirical investigations, and generating new areas of research (e.g., the impact of technology on translation practice and pedagogy, human-machine interaction, evaluation of tools).

FURTHER READING

- Kingscott (1996) presents a general discussion of the impact of technology and its implications for teaching translation.
- Topping (2000a) discusses the pressure placed on translators to work faster, better, and more cost-effectively, and presents a case study that focuses on shortening the translation cycle with the help of technology.
- Kenny (1999) provides an overview of the benefits and implications associated with the use of CAT tools in an academic environment.
- DeCesaris (1996) describes how translation-memory systems can be used as teaching aids.
- De Schaetzen (1997) investigates the type of knowledge that students need to have about computerized terminology tools and explores a number of different options for integrating such tools into the classroom.
- L'Homme (1999b) outlines how a variety of CAT tools have been integrated into the translator-training curriculum at the Université de Montréal.

2. Capturing Data in Electronic Form

We are still far from being a paperless society.

Haynes (1998, 128)

Before you can analyse a text it needs to be in a format in which the computer can recognise it, usually in the format of a standard text file on a storage medium such as a floppy disk or a hard disk. If the text is only currently available in printed or written form this file must be created, since it is not normally convenient, or indeed possible, for the computer to read the data directly from the paper copy.

Barnbrook (1996, 30)

In order for a translator to take advantage of specialized translation technology, the texts to be processed must be in electronic form. It is increasingly common for clients to supply source texts to translators in electronic form (e.g., prepared using a word processor or desktop-publishing package), just as it is increasingly common for translators to be able to find parallel documents in electronic form (e.g., on the World Wide Web or on a CD-ROM). Nevertheless, this is not always the case. A survey undertaken by Webb (1998) reveals that freelance translators still receive approximately 45 percent, and translation agencies approximately 15 percent, of their source texts in hard copy. In addition, translators may wish to convert texts into electronic form in order to compile corpora (see section 3.1), prepare for automatic term extraction (see section 4.4), or build a translation memory (see section 5.2).

In any case, when data are not currently machine-readable (i.e., a document arrives as a fax or a printout), they must be converted. There are two main ways of doing this: using a combination of scanning hardware and optical-character-recognition software and using voice-recognition technology. In addition, even when data arrive in or have been converted to electronic form, they will not necessarily be in a format that is compatible with the technology that the translator wishes to use. Therefore, it may be necessary to convert these data into the appropriate file format.

In this chapter, these technologies will be explained, and the advantages and disadvantages associated with each will be outlined. The purpose of this book is not to overwhelm translators with technical details, but to give them an appreciation of the general approaches used by machines and of the types of difficulties that can be encountered when using technology. By reflecting on the differences between the ways in which humans and machines process data, translators will learn to have more reasonable expectations with regard to the capabilities of technology and how they can interact with machines in order to improve the quality of the machine output.

2.1 Scanning and optical character recognition

One method for converting a hard copy of a text into an electronic copy is to use a piece of hardware called a scanner combined with optical-character-recognition (OCR) software. For the sake of clarity, scanning and OCR will be explained as separate processes; however, in practice, the two can work together in a way that appears seamless to the user.

2.1.1 Scanning

A scanner is a computer peripheral, and there are a variety of models available. These range from small handheld devices, through desktop paper-sized scanners, to large freestanding units.

Handheld scanners are small and lightweight. A user holds the scanner in his or her hand and drags it across the paper. Typically, handheld scanners have a limited scanning window (usually 3 or 4 inches). This means that a user would have to make two or three passes over an ordinary letter-sized page. In addition, the user must have a very steady hand. Handheld scanners are relatively inexpensive, but they are typically too slow and inaccurate to be useful for large amounts of document conversion.

At the other end of the scale, large freestanding units are capable of

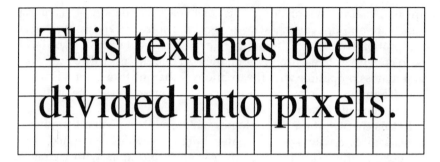

Figure 2.1   A text divided into large pixels. (Normally, the pixels used by a scanner would be much smaller, often on the order of several hundred or even several thousand pixels per square inch.)

processing vast amounts of data quickly and accurately. However, they are quite large and relatively expensive, and they are therefore beyond the means of many translators. Generally, such machines are used by large institutions that have significant scanning needs (e.g., libraries, archives).

In between these two is a third type of scanner, known as a flatbed scanner, which can sit on a desktop and looks a small photocopier. It has a hinged lid, which, when lifted, reveals a glass bed on which a document is placed face down. This is the type of scanner that is best suited to the needs of most translators. It is easy to use and can process reasonable amounts of text fairly quickly and accurately. In addition, many flatbed scanners come with an optional automatic document feeder (like those on photocopiers), which allows users to insert multiple pages to be automatically fed through the scanner one at a time.

Regardless of the model, scanners operate in basically the same way. We will take the flatbed scanner as an example. First, the user places the document to be scanned face down on the glass and closes the lid.

Once the document is in position, the scanner draws an imaginary grid over the document, dividing it up into tiny segments known as pixels. This makes the document appear as if it has been written on fine-grained graph paper, on which each tiny square represents one pixel (see figure 2.1). The greater the number of pixels, the higher the resolution of the scanner, and the sharper the image it will produce. As we will see shortly, the sharpness of the scanned image is important for accurate OCR.

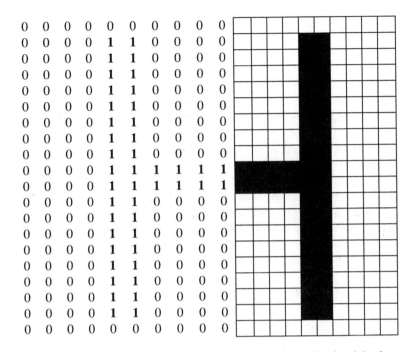

Figure 2.2   The letter "H" divided into pixels. (The left-hand side of the figure shows how the binary digits 0 and 1 are used to record the pattern of reflected light.)

Scanners are optical devices, which means that they operate using light. Lasers are a common light source in many scanners. When the document is in position and the imaginary grid has been drawn, the next step is activation of the light source.

When the light shines on the document, it is reflected back in different intensities using a series of lenses and mirrors. The level of intensity depends on whether the light is being reflected from a black part of the document (an inked character) or a white part of the document (the background paper). (Some scanners are capable of reading colour documents, but for the sake of clarity, we will limit this description to the scanning of a black-and-white document – a page of printed text.)

For each pixel on the document, a sensor generates an electrical voltage according to the intensity of light reflected back from that segment of the document. This voltage is converted into a binary digit that is recorded by the computer (see figure 2.2). If the light reflected from a given pixel is not very bright (i.e., the pixel is on a black part of the document), its intensity is recorded as a 1. If the light reflected from a given pixel is very bright (i.e., the pixel is on a white part of the document), its value is recorded as a 0.

The pattern of 0s and 1s is stored in the computer, which uses this information to re-create an electronic picture of the document that was scanned. It is important to note that at this point in the process, the information is stored as an image or graphic. This essentially means that the computer has taken a picture of the document, but the individual elements of the document (the individual letters or characters in the text) cannot be manipulated separately. In order to convert the picture of the document into usable text (one in which the individual characters can be manipulated using a word processor or other application), a further step is essential, which entails using a piece of software known as OCR software.

2.1.2 Optical character recognition

OCR software takes the scanned image and, through a process of pattern matching, converts the stored image of the text into a form that is truly machine-readable and can be processed by other types of software (e.g., word processors, concordancers, translation memories).

At its most basic, OCR software examines each character in the scanned image and compares it to a series of character patterns stored in a database. When the software perceives that it has made a match, it stores the matched character in a new file and moves on to the next character. Once all the characters in the scanned image have been processed in this way, the new file can be saved in an appropriate format (e.g., as a text file) and opened in an application such as a word processor, where it can be edited or manipulated as desired.

2.1.2.1 Factors affecting the accuracy of OCR

Not surprisingly, there is scope for error during the character-recognition process. Sometimes the OCR software makes an incorrect match. For instance, the letter "e" might be mistaken for a "c," the number "5" might be mistaken for the letter "S," or the letters "c" and "l" might be mistakenly combined to form a "d." A number of factors can affect the accuracy of OCR, one of the most important being the quality of the

This is a clear, crisp text that is suitable for use with OCR software.	This text is faded and somewhat blurred and is not a good candidate for use with OCR software.	This text contains a coffee-ring stain that will distort certain characters in the text when it is processed by the OCR software.	This **text** is written using a variety of different **FONTS** and is **not** a good *candidate* for use with *OCR software.*

Figure 2.3   Sample texts of differing quality.

hard copy. On the one hand, if the document being scanned is faded (e.g., a poor-quality photocopy or fax), the intensity of the light that is reflected from the faded characters may be too similar to the level of intensity that is reflected from the background. In such circumstances, the OCR software does not pick out all the characters. On the other hand, if the document is blurred, smudged, stained, or creased, parts of it that should actually comprise the background may be incorrectly recognized as characters. Other factors include the size and style of the font on the page (e.g., small characters and characters in fancy scripts are more difficult to process, as are texts that contain a mixture of fonts), the layout of the text (e.g., columns and tables can be difficult to process), and the character set used (e.g., it may be necessary to purchase different OCR packages to process different languages or to handle texts containing mathematical formulas). For the best results, texts should be clean original laser printouts with limited formatting. A selection of texts of differing qualities is shown in figure 2.3.

Sophisticated OCR packages use more complex processing techniques than those described here. One replacement for the classic approach described here, which focuses on isolated characters, is a technique that makes use of context. For example, if an OCR system looked at the surrounding characters before making a decision, it would be easier to tell that the first character in the string "Sir" should be interpreted as the letter "S" and not as the number "5." Another technique is to integrate a dictionary checking stage. For example, if a pattern is initially interpreted as "hcuse," a dictionary check would reveal that this is not a legitimate combination and would suggest viable alternatives, such as "house." This is similar to the way many spellchecker programs work in word-processing packages. It does not, however, solve all misinterpretation problems. For example, if an OCR program mistakenly identifies the "e" in "read" as an "o," the resulting word will be "road," which will not be identified as an error during a dictionary check because "road" is a legitimate word. In the future, OCR software may need to take even larger contexts into account – perhaps parsing entire sentences in order to determine whether a given word makes sense in this larger context.

2.1.3 Benefits and drawbacks of scanning and OCR

There are a number of benefits to be gained by using scanning and OCR to convert documents into electronic form, but this approach is not without some drawbacks. Translators will have to weigh its advantages and disadvantages in the light of their own situation (budget, language combination, volume of data to be converted, etc.).

2.1.3.1 Injury

One main advantage of scanning and OCR is that it allows a translator to take a document that is currently available only in hard copy and convert it into electronic form without having to type it in. The fact that a user does not have to type means that there will be a reduced risk of injuries such as repetitive strain injury or carpal-tunnel syndrome, which are associated with keyboarding.

2.1.3.2 Time

Another disadvantage of keyboarding is that keyboard entry by non-professional typists is typically slower than OCR. If the work is contracted out to a professional typist, it can be costly. If there are a considerable number of documents to be entered, there is a good chance that the cost of the scanner and OCR software will be lower than the cost of hiring someone to do data entry, with the added bonus that the computer equipment will still be available the next time hard-copy documents need to be converted. On the other hand, keyboard entry is often more accurate than OCR, so time gained during the scanning/OCR process may later need to be invested in proofreading and editing.

2.1.3.3 Quality

Some OCR packages make claims of up to 99 percent accuracy; however, in practice, such rates are rarely achieved. As mentioned above, the accuracy of OCR depends heavily on the quality of the document being scanned. OCR works well for good-quality, straightforward printed originals, but if the document is faded, blurred, creased, or heavily formatted, or if it contains foreign characters or mathematical formulas, the results will likely be less accurate. Similarly, handwritten texts are problematic. Although efforts are underway to develop OCR systems that can recognize handwritten texts, the accuracy of such systems is often low, which is understandable given the wide range of handwriting styles that exist. However, there has been some success developing systems that can be "trained" to recognize the handwriting of specific users. Because OCR is not perfect, texts that are converted using this technology will need to be closely proofread and edited, and this can be a time-consuming process.

2.1.3.4 Languages and file formats

Another important point is that most OCR systems work for particular languages, which means that a translator may have to invest in one software package for each working language. Some multilingual products are available for certain language combinations; however, these packages may not include all the languages required by a given translator.

In addition, it is important to remember that not all OCR software works directly with all other software applications. Some OCR packages allow users to save files into certain formats (e.g., for use with a specific word processor). In other cases, text that is scanned using OCR may later need to be converted into a different format in order to be edited or processed using a different software application. More details on file formats and conversion are provided in section 2.3.

2.1.3.5 Economic aspects

The cost of scanners and OCR software has dropped considerably and these products are now within the budget of many translators. Prices range from around a hundred dollars up to several thousand dollars. Furthermore, this technology does not necessarily require the translator's computer to be equipped with a significant amount of memory or processing power, though certain products may require higher specifications than others. Individual translators will have to weigh the cost against the anticipated frequency of use of the technology. In addition, as might be expected, the accuracy of this technology typically increases in proportion to the price. Experience has shown that while translators can generally make due with a relatively inexpensive scanner, it is worth their while to invest in good OCR software because cheaper software may not seem such a bargain if they have to spend an inordinate amount of time editing the output. Finally, as previously mentioned, some OCR packages work for only one language (or a restricted set of languages), so translators working with multiple languages may need to purchase several OCR packages. Details on a number of commercially available OCR packages can be found in Appendix B.

2.2 Voice recognition

Voice recognition, also known as speech recognition, is a technology that allows a user to interact with a computer by speaking to it instead of using a keyboard or mouse. This technology has been in development since the 1950s, but getting a computer to recognize human language is a very complex task, and only recently has voice recognition become widely available. The popularity of voice-recognition software has been spurred by two main factors: the hardware required to implement this technology can now be integrated into desktop computers, and these computers have become more affordable.

Voice-recognition software basically works as follows. The user speaks into a microphone, which is linked to a sound card inside the computer. The software acoustically analyzes the speech input by breaking down the sounds that the hardware "hears" into smaller, indivisible sounds called phonemes (distinct units of sound). In languages that use a phonemic writing system, phonemes can be thought of as the sound made by a letter or small group of letters. For example, the English word "those" is made up of three phonemes: the "th" sound, the long "o" sound, and the "z" sound made by the "se" combination. Phonemes can be combined to form syllables, syllables make up words, and words form sentences.

Once the software has broken sounds into phonemes and syllables, a "best guess" algorithm is used to map the phonemes and syllables into words. The computer's guesses are then compared against a database of stored word patterns. Most software comes with a base vocabulary already in the database, along with a facility for allowing the user to add to this database. Additional specialized glossaries (e.g., glossaries of medical or legal terms) can also be purchased for some systems.

Voice-recognition software also uses grammatical context and frequency to predict possible words. These statistical tools reduce the amount of time it takes the software to search through the database. Strings of words are parsed into logical units based on context, speech patterns, and more "best guess" algorithms. Such strategies allow some systems to try to differentiate between homophones – words that sound the same but are spelled differently and have different meanings (e.g., "to," "too," "two") – for example. Based on the surrounding context, a voice-recognition system may try to guess which of the homophones is the intended word in a given context, though it may not always guess correctly. For example, it may seem to be a logical "best guess" that the form that should precede the word "many" is "too" (e.g., "There are too many people in the room"). Although this may be correct in many instances, there will be some occasions where it is the incorrect choice (e.g., "The accusation seemed absurd to many people" or "Now it takes me five minutes to run 500 metres, but it only took me two many years ago").

It is worth pointing out that although voice-recognition technology has been developed for a variety of different languages, not all languages are equally conducive to being recognized by a computer. It is more difficult for a computer to recognize languages that contain a great deal of elision or liaison (when words seem to "run together" or blend into one another without distinct pauses between them). In French, for example, the computer may have difficulty distinguishing between the word "laide" and the form "l'aide," which is produced by elision. Similarly, the use of liaison in French means that in cases where a word begins with a vowel (e.g., "aidez"), the final consonant of the preceding word, which may not normally be pronounced, is pronounced and blended with the vowel so that the two words no longer have a pause between them (e.g., "vous_aidez").

2.2.1 Types of voice-recognition technology

Different types of voice-recognition packages have different degrees of functionality: speaker-dependent vs. speaker-independent systems, command/control vs. dictation systems, and discrete vs. continuous systems.

A voice-recognition dictation system that is speaker dependent requires a user to "train" the software before it can be used. Therefore, this type of system is sometimes called a trained voice-recognition system. Training consists of reading through a manufacturer-provided list of words or sentences that contain all the different sounds in a language. Often the user is required to pronounce each word on the list several times before moving on to the next word. Altogether, the training can take several hours to complete. Once the training exercise is complete, the computer makes calculations based on the voice data that it has received. These calculations are used to draw up a voice profile that matches the speaker's vocal patterns. No two speakers sound exactly the same (we have different pitches, tones, accents), and a speaker-dependent system that has been trained by user A cannot then be used successfully by user B. In order for user B to be able to work with the system, he or she must also complete the training exercise and create his or her own voice profile.

In contrast, speaker-independent voice-recognition technology, also known as universal voice recognition, does not require user training. Typically, the manufacturers have "pre-trained" the software using speech samples from a wide range of people. Therefore, a user may begin using a speaker-independent voice-recognition program upon installation. At first glance, speaker-independent systems seem like a good option; however, if the user's voice patterns fall outside the sample range (e.g., if the user speaks with a foreign accent), it may be difficult to get the system to work properly. On the other hand, even speaker-dependent systems that have been trained to recognize the voice of a specific user may not work all the time. For example, if the user has a head cold, his or her pronunciation may temporarily change and may not be recognized by the system.

Another distinction between voice-recognition systems is whether they are command/control systems or dictation systems. Command/control systems allow users to interact with the computer by giving a limited set of commands, which usually correspond to the commands found on application menus (e.g., "Open," "Copy," "Paste"). In contrast, dictation systems allow users to enter new data into the computer by dictating instead of typing. Command/control systems cannot be used to convert a printed text into electronic form; this process requires a dictation system. Some hybrid products combine both command/control and dictation features into a single system.

Systems that allow dictation can be further broken down into discrete (or interrupted) speech vs. continuous-speech systems. With a discrete system, the user must pause between words so that the computer can distinguish where one word ends and the next begins. For most speakers, this entails modifying their normal way of speaking, reducing it to a slower and more stilted pace. Some ... users ... find ... this ... difficult ... or ... frustrating. In contrast, a continuous-speech system allows users to speak at a more normal pace, though pronunciation must still be very clear.

2.2.2 Tips for improving the accuracy of voice-recognition technology

While the quality of voice-recognition software is improving steadily, many users still experience problems with accuracy because of the language in question, the manner in which they speak, or the nature of their voice: some languages and speech patterns are simply more difficult for the computer to interpret than others. This means that texts that are converted into electronic form using voice-recognition software must be proofread carefully. Nevertheless, there are a number of ways in which translators can help to improve the accuracy of these systems.

First, when using speaker-dependent systems, translators must be certain to train the system using their normal speaking voice; there is no point in training the system when you have a head cold or a sore throat. The translator must then use his or her normal voice when interacting with the system – the system will not recognize the translator's voice if he or she is whispering or shouting. Sometimes, when the system fails to recognize a word correctly, users can get frustrated and raise their voice or begin talking in a strained and angry way. This change in voice pattern means the software is even less likely to recognize the words, and the user may become even more frustrated and eventually stop using the system.

Another important tip for improving accuracy is to enunciate words clearly. The software will recognize the words that the translator actually says, which may not be the words that the translator meant to say. For instance, if a translator wants to say "off and on," but fails to enunciate clearly, the voice recognition package may recognize the pattern as "often on." Similarly, the word "wander" could be mistaken for "wonder" if the pronunciation is not clear. While human beings can generally use situational context and real-world understanding to correctly interpret utterances, a machine has no idea that in the context of a document on transportation, the utterance "next train" makes more sense than "neck strain" – it simply transcribes what it hears. Translators should not litter their dictation with sighs, throat-clearing noises, or hesitation noises, such as "um" or "uh," as these may be picked up by the system and inserted into the text. Some voice-recognition systems can play back an audio version of what the speaker actually said, and this can be useful for trying to identify the cause of an error.

Voice-recognition technology should be used in a quiet room where there is little background noise. Depending on the sensitivity of the software, some background noises may distort the speech patterns that the computer hears. Therefore, open-plan or shared offices may not be the best place to use voice-recognition systems.

In this section, voice recognition has been presented as a technology that can be used for converting existing hard-copy texts into electronic form so that they can be processed by CAT tools such as concordancers and translation-memory systems. However, there is another way in which many translators may be interested in using voice recognition: for composing new target texts. Some translators may find it more convenient to dictate a new translation, rather than type it. Some experienced translators may already be familiar with the practice of dictating translations (e.g., using dictation machines) and they may prefer to work in this way, finding that they can produce higher-quality texts more quickly. However, for many new translators, composing while dictating will represent a new skill to be learned. One trick for improving the accuracy of voice-recognition technology while dictating is for translators to think about what they are going to say before they say it. If people talk without thinking, they may find that words get mumbled as they change their mind midway through a sentence. Whatever the speaker says will be captured by the voice-recognition system, and poorly composed texts will need to be edited more heavily at a later stage.

2.2.3 Benefits and drawbacks of voice-recognition technology

Voice-recognition technology is one of the most exciting technologies on the market today, but as well as offering a number of advantages, this technology also has a number of shortcomings. The benefits and drawbacks of using a voice-recognition system must be weighed by translators in the light of their own working situation.

2.2.3.1 Injury

As with OCR, one of the greatest advantages of voice recognition is that users do not have to use a keyboard. For users who are poor typists, or who suffer from a physical or visual impairment or a repetitive strain injury, voice recognition offers an alternative to keyboarding. Because users do not need to sit directly in front of a computer in order to dictate, they can assume a working position that is more comfortable, which may help to alleviate back and neck problems caused by hunching over a keyboard. It is important to note, however, that vocal cords are also subject to injury. Most translators are not used to speaking for eight hours a day, and launching into this type of working style can put a serious strain on vocal cords, which may result in temporary laryngitis or more permanent injuries. Translators who elect to work with voice-recognition technology are generally advised to take regular breaks and drink plenty of water.

2.2.3.2 Time

In addition to working more comfortably, some users find that dictation allows them to work more quickly. Because many users can speak more quickly than they can type, they can process a greater volume of text when dictating. Furthermore, keyboarding is a very hands-on operation, whereas talking into a microphone leaves your hands free to leaf through the reference material that you have on your desk while translating. However, keep in mind that time gained during the initial composition phase may need to be invested in proofreading and editing the text to correct errors made by the voice-recognition technology.

Finally, as mentioned above, most voice-recognition packages come with a base dictionary of general vocabulary. Given that the bulk of translation takes place in specialized fields, translators may have to spend a considerable amount of time augmenting the dictionaries to include specialized terms. Doctors and lawyers were among the first clients targeted by voice-recognition software developers because these professionals do a considerable amount of dictation. Therefore, there are numerous specialized add-on dictionaries available in the fields of medicine and law, so translators working in these fields may be able to take advantage of these ready-made dictionaries. Dictionaries in other fields, such as insurance and accounting, are becoming more common, but many translators will need to build their own dictionaries to reflect their own areas of specialization.

2.2.3.3 Quality

Issues relating to the quality of voice-recognition software have been largely discussed in section 2.2.2. Basically, the quality of the output depends largely on the quality of the input – translators must be prepared to speak slowly and clearly. In general, the output of trained speaker-dependent systems tends to be of a higher quality than that of speaker-independent systems.

2.2.3.4 Languages and file formats

It is worth noting that because phonemes differ from language to language, voice-recognition systems work for specific languages, which means that a translator may have to invest in multiple packages – one for each working language. In addition, not all voice-recognition packages work directly with all other software applications. Some systems can be integrated with specific word processors (e.g., MS Word, Word-Perfect), which means that as the translator dictates, the text is entered directly into that word processor. Other systems use proprietary text editors, which means that text dictated into the system will later need to be converted into a different format in order to be edited or processed using a different software application. More details on file formats and conversion are provided in section 2.3.

2.2.3.5 Integration with other tools

It has just been noted that some voice-recognition software can be integrated with word-processing packages; however, another, more exciting type of integration is currently being explored. A number of research groups are investigating the integration of voice-recognition software with machine-translation systems and speech synthesizers. This research could eventually result in the production of simultaneous-interpretation machines! Essentially, a user speaks into a voice-recognition system, which converts speech to text as described above. The source text is then processed by a machine-translation system and the target-text output can either be read on a computer screen by a human, or fed into a speech synthesizer, which reads the text aloud in a computer-generated voice. Of course, there are many challenges still to be overcome (e.g., real-time processing, recognition of emotion), but it is an exciting prospect for the future.

2.2.3.6 Economic aspects

Like OCR software, voice-recognition software is dropping in price and is now reasonably affordable. However, users should remember that in addition to the software, it is necessary to have a computer equipped with a sound card and microphone, as well as a considerable amount of memory and storage capacity. The price also depends on the type of system required, with speaker-independent continuous-speech systems being the most expensive. In addition, as previously mentioned, voice-recognition software is language-dependent, which means that translators wishing to dictate in multiple languages will need to purchase multiple packages. Finally, although base dictionaries come with the software, specialized add-on dictionaries must usually be purchased separately. Descriptions of a number of commercially available voice-recognition products can be found in Appendix B.

2.3 File formats and file conversion

The two preceding sections have focused on ways of getting hard copies of documents into electronic form. However, the simple fact that a document is in electronic form, whether it has been created electronically or converted using OCR or voice-recognition technology, does not necessarily mean that the data will be compatible with the software applications (e.g., concordancer, term-extraction tool, translation-memory system) that a translator may wish to use in order to further process these data.

Different software applications represent and store information in different ways, and this results in the creation of different file formats. The type of file format is often indicated by the filename extension. For instance, a .doc extension indicates that the file was created using MS Word; a .wpd extension indicates that a file was created using Word-Perfect; a .pdf extension is used for Adobe Acrobat files; and an .html file is one that can be read using an Internet browser such as Netscape's Navigator or Microsoft's Internet Explorer. Certain file formats are proprietary and can therefore be read only by a copy of the application that was used to create the file in the first place, whereas other file formats, such as the American Standard Code for Information Interchange (ASCII), can be read by many different applications. ASCII files can be processed by many different applications because the ASCII format has been developed as a recognized standard. In addition, ASCII files are basically plain text files that contain little or no formatting. The more complex the document (the more formatting and special features that it contains), the less likely that it can be successfully opened by another application. Table 2.1 contains a brief description of some types of file formats that are commonly encountered by translators, as well as an indication of problems that might be associated with converting files between these different formats. Although the focus in table 2.1 is on text-based formats, it should be noted that there are many other types of file formats (e.g., .bmp, .gif and .jpg for graphics; .wav for sound files; .avi for videos), and translators who work with multimedia documents (e.g., Web pages) will need to be familiar with these too.

Essentially, it is important to be aware of the fact that translators receive source texts in a variety of different file formats, and their clients typically want to receive the translated text back in the format in which the source text was sent. In order to be able to import files from and export files to other formats, applications must be equipped with filters or converters – one for each different file format. Unfortunately, no application comes equipped with a filter for every file format in existence, so before accepting work from a client, the translator must be sure that the file in question can be opened and processed using the available software.

Another problem associated with some filters is that information may be lost during the import or export process (see table 2.1). Often, some formatting information will be lost; sometimes, the actual content can also go astray. A good filter will attempt to ensure that neither the content nor the formatting information is lost. Unfortunately, filters do not always work perfectly, and translators should test them carefully before exchanging files with clients or colleagues.

When no suitable filters are provided within an application, it may be possible to find a stand-alone conversion program that can be used to convert a file into the desired format. Such programs can be used, for example, to convert files between different application formats, as well as between different types of computer systems, such as IBM-compatible and Macintosh. Appendix B provides details on some commercially available conversion programs.

Finally, it is worth mentioning two other types of files that translators may encounter: compressed files (also known as zipped files) and encoded files. Compression and encoding are processes that can be applied to almost any type of file format. File-compression programs have two main uses. First, they can be used to reduce the size of file by eliminating data redundancies, which exist in all types of files. The advantage of this is that smaller files can be transferred more quickly (and therefore more cheaply) across a network. Second, they allow users to combine several individual files into one compressed file, which is typically referred to as an archive. This means that related documents, or even different parts of a single document that have been created as separate files (e.g., text and graphics files), can be packaged together and shipped as a single file. Most compression programs also come with a decompression feature that restores files to their original form. The extension of a compressed file will depend on the compression software that is used, but one of the most common compression programs is WinZip, which has a .zip extension.

Encoded files, such as those with .mim (MIME), .uue (UUencoded) or .bin (BinHex) extensions, are generally encountered as e-mail attachments. Internet mail was originally designed for ASCII text, but, as we have seen, attachments can be created using a variety of different software packages that have proprietary formats. The main reason for encoding a file is to ensure that characters (particularly accented characters or special symbols) are preserved. When a file is encoded, it is converted into ASCII text, which can then be safely transmitted as an e-mail attachment. This may seem to contradict what is stated above and in table 2.1 – that ASCII does not support a wide range of special characters – however, when a file is encoded, a combination of ASCII characters may be used to represent a single special character (e.g., "ŵ" may be represented as "w^" or "Φ" may be represented as "Io"). The file will need to be decoded by the recipient in order to restore it to its original format. Many e-mail programs carry out this encoding and decoding automatically without the user having to intervene. However, standalone encoding/decoding software is also available.

KEY POINTS

- For translators to be able to use CAT tools, data must be in machine-readable form, but many translators still receive a substantial number of their source texts in hard copy.
- There are two main technologies used for converting printed text into electronic text: OCR and voice recognition.
- OCR software takes a scanned image and, through a process of pattern matching, converts the stored image of the text into a form that is truly machine-readable and can be processed by other types of software (e.g., CAT tools).

Table 2.1 Different file formats and some associated conversion problems

Format	Description	Potential problems	Sample text	Comments on sample text conversion
Proprietary formats such as **MS Word files (.doc)** or **WordPerfect files (.wpd)**	Files created and saved using specific applications, such as MS Word or WordPerfect, are stored in proprietary formats. The formats used by high-end word processors typically support a wide range of fonts, characters, and formatting, including complex formatting such as tables, lists, footnotes, and hyperlinks.	Because these formats are proprietary, files created using applications such as MS Word or WordPerfect cannot easily be opened using other applications. In order to view a proprietary file using another application, the file must typically be converted to another format (e.g., .rtf, .html, or .txt) and some information, particularly complex formatting information, may be lost during the conversion process.	This sample text includes a variety of different features: • **bold**, *italics*, and <u>underlining</u> • *different STYLES* of fonts • foreign characters (âëîöüÿWø) • mathematical symbols (∑π∞) • a hyperlink <u>mail@mailbox.com</u>	The sample text to the left is the original text that was created using MS Word. It contains a variety of formatting features and special characters.
Rich Text Format files (.rtf) Most word processors have a "Save As" conversion option that allows files to be saved in .rtf format	RTF (Rich Text Format) is a file format that allows the user to transfer formatted text and graphics from one word processor to another. The RTF specification defines control words and symbols that serve as "common denominator" formatting commands. For example, when saving an MS Word file in RTF, the proprietary markup language used by MS Word is translated into to the RTF language. When this RTF file is opened by another application, such as WordPerfect, the RTF language is then translated into the proprietary markup language used by WordPerfect.	RTF supports most basic formatting features (e.g., bold, italics, centring), but it may have difficulty accurately converting more complex formatting features such as lists, tables, footnotes and hyperlinks.	This sample text includes a variety of different features: • **bold**, *italics*, and <u>underlining</u> • διϕϕεριϛ styles of *fonts* • foreign characters (âëîöüÊï_) • mathematical symbols (x_J) • a hyperlink <u>mail@mailbox.com</u>	The original MS Word text was saved in Rich Text Format and then re-opened in WordPerfect. Some of the formatting features and special characters have been lost or distorted.

Table 2.1 (Concluded)

Format	Description	Potential problems	Sample text	Comments on sample text conversion
HyperText Markup Language files (.html) Many word processors have a "Save As" conversion option that allows files to be saved in .html format	HTML (HyperText Markup Language) is the set of markup symbols or codes inserted in a file intended for display on a World Wide Web browser page. The markup tells the browser how to display a Web page's words and images for the user. Each individual markup code is referred to as a tag. Some tags come in pairs that indicate where a display effect (e.g., bold, italics) begins and ends.	HTML supports an extremely wide range of formatting, fonts, and character sets; however, depending on the application that you use to open an HTML file, you may end up seeing all the tags, which makes the text difficult to read.	Viewed using a browser: This sample text includes a variety of different features: • **bold**, *italics* and <u>underlining</u> • ***different STYLES*** of fonts • foreign characters (âêïöûỳẁ∅) • mathematical symbols (Σπ∞) • a hyperlink mail@mailbox.com Viewed as a source file (extract): \<p class=MsoNormal>\<span lang=EN-IE style='font-size:12.0pt;mso-ansi-language: EN-IE'>This sample text includes a variety of different features: \<o:p>\</o:p>\</span> \</p> \<p class=MsoNormal style='margin-left:.25in;text-indent:-.25in;	The original MS Word text was saved as an HTML file. When viewed using a browser, all the formatting and special characters have been preserved. However, when viewed as a source file, all the tags are visible which makes reading the text difficult.
ASCII or plain text files (.txt) Most word processors have a "Save As" option that allows files to be saved as .txt files	ASCII is a very basic file format. In an ASCII file, each alphabetic, numeric, and special character is represented with a 7-bit number, which means that a total of 128 characters are defined. In extended ASCII, 8-bits are used, which means that an additional 128 characters can be defined (e.g., additional symbols and foreign characters) for a total of 256 characters. ASCII is not capable of representing different fonts or displaying formatting information (e.g., bold, italics, tables, footnotes).	ASCII is a commonly recognized character set in a variety of applications because it is very basic. ASCII does not support formatting and only supports a limited number foreign characters and special symbols.	```This sample text includes a variety of different features: * bold, italics and underlining * different styles of fonts * foreign characters (àéïöû(()) * mathematical symbols ((()) * a hyperlink mail@mailbox.com```	The original MS Word text was saved as an ASCII file, but all formatting features (e.g., bold, italics) have been lost, the text is displayed in a single font (Courier), and many of the special symbols are not represented because they are not included in the ASCII character set.

- In order to improve the accuracy of OCR, documents should be of high quality (not faded, creased or smudged) and should not contain complex formatting.
- Voice-recognition software allows a user to speak to a computer. There are several types of voice-recognition software, but the majority of translators will likely be most interested in systems that allow continuous speech dictation. Such systems can be either speaker dependent (i.e., each individual user needs to train the system on his or her own computer) or speaker independent.
- In order to enhance the quality of voice-recognition software, users should speak in their normal voice and try to enunciate clearly.
- The fact that data are in electronic form does not necessarily mean that they will be compatible with all software applications. Different software applications represent and store information in different ways, and this results in the creation of different file formats.
- Filters or conversion programs can be used to convert files between different application formats, but such programs do not always work perfectly and there is a risk that data may be distorted or lost.

FURTHER READING

- Haynes (1998, chapter 12) gives a general description of scanning and OCR, while Belaïd (1998, section 2.3) describes more advanced techniques used in OCR.
- L'Homme (1999a, chapter 6) outlines the steps involved in scanning and OCR and discusses some of the factors affecting the quality of the output.
- Barnbrook (1996) discusses difficulties associated with scanning and OCR (chapter 2, section 3.2.1), keyboard entry (chapter 2, section 3.2.2), and voice recognition (chapter 7, section 8).
- Norton and Goodman (1997) explain how voice-recognition technology works (chapter 19). They also present information about file formats and conversion (chapter 9) and file compression (chapter 10).
- Samuelsson-Brown (1996) discusses the use of voice-recognition technology in a translation environment.
- Haynes (1998, chapter 2) gives a general overview of the current state of the art with regard to the integration of voice-recognition, machine-translation, and speech-synthesis systems, while Rayner et al. (2000) and Wahlster (2000) provide more technical descriptions of two such projects.

3. Corpora and Corpus-Analysis Tools

Putting a word in context means breathing life into it. ... If you want to know how words behave you must study them in their natural environment, and the natural environment of words is text, context.

Roumen and van der Ster (1993, 215)

In its broadest sense, a corpus is simply a collection of texts or utterances that is used as a basis for conducting some type of linguistic investigation. Corpus-based research using printed corpora has a very long history within the discipline of translation. Translators generally compile and analyze corpora when conducting terminological research. In addition, when translating a document, translators typically gather and consult corpora of parallel texts (texts that have the same communicative function as the source text but have been written independently in the target language) for guidance with regard to appropriate style, format, terminology, and phraseology.

In spite of the valuable information they contain, printed corpora have a number of shortcomings. First, the effort required to physically gather a printed corpus often entails spending hours at the library and/or photocopier. Once the printed corpus is gathered, further hours must be spent consulting the texts, which often means reading through much irrelevant material before stumbling upon a sought-after term or a discussion of a pertinent point. Furthermore, it is rarely sufficient to consult only one or two parallel texts. Because translators are not necessarily subject-field experts, they must consult a selection of texts in order to ensure that the style and terminology that they adopt are generally accepted by the experts in the field and not simply the idiosyncratic usage of a single author. In addition, it can be difficult to detect patterns of linguistic and stylistic generality when their occurrences are pages, or even documents, apart. Thus, acquiring and working with printed corpora has two major disadvantages. The first is that when working manually, the translator cannot typically gather and consult a wide enough range of documents to ensure that all the relevant concepts, terms, and linguistic patterns will be present. Second, manual analysis is inherently error-prone: the unaided human mind simply cannot discover all the significant patterns, let alone organize them in meaningful ways. The more time spent gathering and consulting a corpus, the less time remains for the task of translation. When translators are working to meet a tight deadline, it can be difficult for them to achieve the correct balance between corpus gathering and consultation on the one hand, and the actual task of translation on the other.

3.1 Electronic corpora

Recently, the term "corpus" has come to refer specifically to a large collection of electronic texts that have been gathered according to explicit criteria. There are three important characteristics to note here: "large," "electronic," and "explicit criteria."

Because machine-readable texts can often be gathered and consulted more quickly than can printed texts, an electronic corpus is typically much larger than a printed corpus. The term "large" is rather vague, but there are no hard-and-fast rules about exactly how large a corpus needs to be. It depends very much on the project at hand, and translators must use the same judgment with regard to appropriate quality and quantity as they would when compiling a printed corpus. The main thing to note here is that given a fixed period of time, a translator working with an electronic corpus will likely be able to consult a wider range of documents than will a translator working with a printed corpus.

The advantage of compiling a corpus in electronic form is that the data can then be manipulated by a computer. Some texts are created directly in electronic form (e.g., using a word processor). Electronic texts can be exchanged on diskettes or downloaded from the World Wide Web or from CD-ROMs. When texts have not been created in electronic form or the electronic version is not available, printed texts can be converted into electronic form using technology such as OCR or voice recognition (see sections 2.1 and 2.2). Once an electronic corpus has been created, special software packages known as corpus-analysis tools can be used to help the translator manipulate the data. These tools allow the translator to access and display the information contained within the corpus in a variety of useful ways, which are described in sections 3.2.1 to 3.2.3. It is very important to note, however, that these tools do not interpret the data – it is still the responsibility of the translator to analyze the information found in the corpus.

Finally, it must be pointed out that a corpus is not simply a random collection of texts. Rather, the texts are selected according to explicit criteria in order to be used as a representative sample of a particular language or subset of that language. Just as a translator would carefully review any texts that were to be included in a printed corpus, so must the translator evaluate texts to be included in an electronic corpus. For example, a translator building an electronic corpus might wish to include only texts that deal with a given topic, are of a certain text type, and were produced within a certain time frame. In this way, translators can build different electronic corpora for different projects, just as they would collect different printed corpora for use with different projects. As explained in the introduction, corpus design is a very important step; however, design issues are somewhat independent from the technology used to manipulate a corpus. The focus of this book is technology, but readers interested in learning more about corpus design issues can consult works such as Engwall (1994), Bowker (1996), Meyer and Mackintosh (1996), Pearson (1998), Austermühl (2001), and Bowker and Pearson (2002).

3.1.1 Some different types of electronic corpora

Given that corpora are specially designed to meet the needs of the project at hand, there are as many different corpora as there are projects. Nevertheless, it is possible to identify some general characteristics that corpora may have. For instance, corpora can be monolingual, bilingual, or multilingual. A monolingual corpus is one that contains texts in a single language. Bilingual and multilingual corpora contain texts in two or more languages, respectively. Most commonly, such corpora will contain texts in language A alongside their translations into language B, language C, and so on. A bilingual corpus that contains source texts and their translations is sometimes referred to as bitext, but the more common term is parallel corpus, which can be used to describe both bilingual and multilingual collections. Unfortunately, there can be some confusion surrounding the word "parallel." As described above, the printed parallel texts conventionally used by translators consist of texts that have the same communicative function as the source text, but that were originally written in the target language; in other words, they are not translations of the source text but are texts of the same text type, on the same topic, and so on. Parallel corpora, on the other hand, consist of source texts aligned with their translations. The notion of alignment is an important one if the parallel corpus is to be optimally useful. Alignment is discussed in greater detail in section 3.2.2.2.

Other types of corpora include monolingual comparable corpora and bilingual comparable corpora. Monolingual comparable corpora consist of two parts: a collection of texts that have been originally written in language A, and a collection of texts that have been translated into language A from other languages. This type of corpus is useful for researchers interested in studying the nature of translated text; however, it is less useful as a resource for practising translators. Bilingual comparable corpora are akin to the printed parallel texts used by translators: both parts of this corpus contain texts that are of the same text type and on the same subject, but one collection contains texts originally written in language A while the other collection contains texts originally written in language B. Because the two collections do not have a source text-target text relationship, they cannot be aligned. Therefore, although a bilingual comparable corpus contains a potential wealth of useful information for translators, it is very difficult to identify and retrieve the relevant sections of the text in a semi-automated way. A great deal of active research is being carried out with regard to the development and exploitation of monolingual and bilingual comparable corpora, so it may not be long before tools for helping translators to exploit these resources become available. For more information on monolingual comparable corpora, see Baker (1996) and Laviosa (1998); for further details on bilingual comparable corpora, see Bennison and Bowker (2000).

3.2 Corpus-analysis tools

Although there are some differences between printed and electronic corpora, in many respects, the use of an electronic corpus is not so much a radical departure from the use of a printed corpus, but a refinement that allows translators to take advantage of the benefits offered by electronic media. In order to do this, translators need access to computerized tools that will help them manipulate and investigate the contents of the corpus. Such tools let users access and display the information contained within a corpus in a variety of useful ways. Most corpus-analysis tools typically contain a number of useful features that allow users to generate and manipulate word-frequency lists, concordances, and collocations. These features are described below.

It is also worth pointing out that many corpus-analysis tools were not developed specifically for translators. Initially, such tools were intended for use by other language professionals, including foreign-language teachers and lexicographers. Nevertheless, they are becoming increasingly popular with translators and terminologists, primarily because they allow users to have access to frequency data and to see terms in a variety of contexts simultaneously – features that dictionaries and printed corpora cannot easily provide.

3.2.1 Word-frequency lists

The most basic feature provided by a corpus-analysis tool is a word-frequency list, which allows users to discover how many different words are in a corpus and how often each appears. These two figures are referred to as types and tokens. For illustrative purposes, suppose that a corpus consists of the following sentence:

I really like translation because I think that translation is really, really fun.

This sentence contains a total of thirteen words; therefore, the corpus contains thirteen tokens. However, some of the words appear more than once (I, really, translation); therefore, the corpus contains only nine *different* words, and these are known as types. In a word-frequency list, the types are presented in a list and the number of tokens (the number of times that word occurs) is shown beside the type. This is illustrated in figure 3.1.

Word-frequency lists can be manipulated in a number of ways. They can be sorted in various different orders, including order of occurrence in the corpus, alphabetical order, and order of frequency, and these lists can be arranged in ascending or descending order. Therefore, the same

I	2
really	3
like	1
translation	2
because	1
think	1
that	1
is	1
fun	1

Figure 3.1   A word-frequency list showing types on the left and tokens on the right.

I	2	fun	1
really	3	is	1
like	1	that	1
translation	2	think	1
because	1	because	1
think	1	translation	2
that	1	like	1
is	1	really	3
fun	1	I	2

Figure 3.2   Word-frequency lists sorted in order of appearance in the corpus, in descending order (from the beginning of the corpus to the end) and ascending order (from the end of the corpus to the beginning).

word list can be arranged in at least six different ways, as shown in figures 3.2, 3.3, and 3.4.

The single-sentence corpus used in the above examples is purely for illustrative purposes – a translator would not need to use a computerized tool to analyze a single sentence. Normally, a corpus would be much larger – often in the order of hundreds of thousands or even millions of words. In such cases, the advantage of having a computer to help with counting and sorting becomes clear!

In addition to counting the frequency of words, corpus-analysis tools calculate the ratio of types to tokens. Some corpus-analysis tools can also count the number of sentences and paragraphs and calculate

because	1
fun	1
I	2
is	1
like	1
really	3
that	1
think	1
translation	2

translation	2
think	1
that	1
really	3
like	1
is	1
I	2
fun	1
because	1

Figure 3.3   Word-frequency lists sorted in alphabetical order, in descending order (from A to Z) and ascending order (from Z to A).

really	3
I	2
translation	2
because	1
fun	1
is	1
like	1
that	1
think	1

because	1
fun	1
is	1
like	1
that	1
think	1
I	2
translation	2
really	3

Figure 3.4   Word-frequency lists sorted in order of frequency, in descending order (from the most frequent to the least frequent) and ascending order (from the least frequent to the most frequent). When multiple words have the same frequency count, they are further sorted in alphabetical order.

the average length of words, sentences, and paragraphs in the corpus. This type of information can help translators assess some of the stylistic features of the texts in the corpus.

3.2.1.1 Lemmatized lists

Some tools permit more sophisticated types of manipulations, such as the creation of lemmatized lists. A simple word-frequency list will process individual word forms. This means that the words "translate,"

the	1,435
to	800
a	729
and	669
of	633
virus	366
in	357
for	350
is	346
that	323
on	250
it	224
antivirus	209
are	200
viruses	197
be	179
or	178
as	177
with	176
an	152

Figure 3.5   Twenty most frequently occurring types in an unlemmatized corpus.

"translates," "translated," and "translating" are treated as separate forms, even though they are related (they are all inflections of the verb "to translate"). Sometimes, it might be useful for a translator to be able to group related words together to get a combined frequency count for the group of words rather than separate counts for each individual word form. The term "lemma" is normally used to describe a word that includes and represents all related forms. Figure 3.5 contains an extract of the twenty most frequently occurring types (out of a total of 29,589 types) from a corpus containing 183,832 tokens. By looking at a frequency list, users can quickly get a general idea of what the corpus is about.

If this same extract were to be lemmatized, it would appear as shown in figure 3.6. Related words are grouped under a lemma. The total word count for the lemma is shown in the right-hand column,

the		1,435
a		881
	a (729)	
	an (152)	
to		800
be		725
	is (346)	
	are (200)	
	be (179)	
and		669
of		633
virus		563
	virus (366)	
	viruses (197)	
in		357
for		350
that		323
on		250
it		224
antivirus		209
or		178
as		177
with		176

Figure 3.6   A lemmatized word list.

and the frequency counts for the individual words belonging to the lemma are shown in parentheses.

One difficulty that may arise when lemmatizing a word list automatically is the case of homographs. A homograph is a word that has the same spelling as another word but has a different part of speech. For example, the word "test" can be a noun (e.g., "The students wrote the *test*") or a verb (e.g., "The teacher decided to *test* the students"). For some purposes, it may not be desirable to include homographs in the same lemma; however, in order for the computer to be able to distinguish these different forms, it is necessary to have a corpus that is annotated with part-of-speech information. Annotation is discussed in greater detail in section 3.3.

virus	366
is	346
it	224
antivirus	209
are	200
viruses	197
be	179
network	151
you	148
your	138
can	133
email	126
we	125
have	120
software	115
files	109
not	109
said	102
security	93
products	90

Figure 3.7   Twenty most frequently occurring types in a corpus for which a stop list has been implemented.

3.2.1.2 Stop lists

Another type of specialized list is a stop list, which contains any items that a user wants the computer to ignore. For example, translators are often more interested in words that have some semantic content and are less interested in words with a grammatical function, such as articles, conjunctions, and prepositions. If we generate another word-frequency list for the same corpus, but this time using a stop list to ignore function words, the extract of the top twenty words would change as illustrated in figure 3.7. This new frequency list makes it clear that the subject of the corpus in question is computer viruses (as opposed to medical viruses).

   Clearly, the choice of how to sort the lists and the decision about whether or not to use a lemmatized list or a stop list depends on the nature of the information that the user is looking for at a given time. No decision is irreversible: data can be sorted and re-sorted, lemmatization can be implemented and removed, and stop lists can be added, modified, or removed.

3.2.2 Concordancers

Translators not only have to be able to understand the source text, they also have to produce a target text. Tools such as dictionaries are very helpful for comprehension, but in order to be able to determine how terms can be used, it is more useful to see them in context, and, preferably, in more than one context. A second feature that is common to most corpus-analysis tools is a concordancer. Some concordancers operate on monolingual texts, while others operate on bilingual texts, and these will be described separately.

3.2.2.1 Monolingual concordancers

A concordancer is a tool that retrieves all the occurrences of a particular search pattern in its immediate contexts and displays these in an easy-to-read format. Some concordancers operate by searching through the entire corpus from beginning to end every time a search pattern is entered. Others work by first creating an index of all the words in the corpus along with a record of the location of each occurrence (e.g., line number), as illustrated in figure 3.8. The index must be created prior to conducting any searches in a given corpus, but once created, it can be consulted during all subsequent searches for particular items in that corpus.

The advantage of a full-text search is that no pre-processing is required and the corpus can be easily modified (e.g., texts can be added or removed); however, the larger the corpus, the longer a search will take. In contrast, indexed searching requires the preparation of an index ahead of time, but once the index has been created, searches can be conducted relatively quickly, even if the corpus is very large. However, if any changes are made to the corpus, such as the addition or removal of a text, a new index must be created.

Once a search has been conducted, the results are displayed for the user. The most common display format is known as a KWIC ("key word in context") display. In a KWIC display, all occurrences of the search pattern are lined up in the centre of the screen. The extent of the

```
video (2 occurrences)
        occurrence 1: line 53
        occurrence 2: line 724
virus (512 occurrences)
        occurrence 1: line 2
        occurrence 2: line 7
        ...
        occurrence 512: line 12,876
viruses (204 occurrences)
        occurrence 1: line 12
        occurrence 2: line 39
        ...
        occurrence 204: line 978
```

Figure 3.8   A sample extract from an index indicating the words contained in the corpus and the location of each occurrence.

context on either side of the search pattern is variable and can often be specified by the user. The KWIC display in figure 3.9 shows the concordance produced for the search pattern "virus."

As with word-frequency lists, these contexts can be sorted in a variety of ways, such as order of appearance in the corpus (as shown in figure 3.9), or alphabetically according to the words preceding or following the search pattern, as illustrated in figures 3.10 and 3.11.

Sorting the data helps to reveal patterns that might otherwise go undetected. For instance, in the KWIC display sorted according to the word preceding the search pattern (figure 3.10), a cluster of contexts for the multi-word unit "macro virus" is revealed. Similarly, in the KWIC display sorted by the word following the search pattern (figure 3.11), clusters for the multi-word units "virus protection" and "virus signature" come to light.

KWIC displays are not the only type of display available. Often, a translator will need to see a larger context, and concordances can be generated that allow browsing by sentence, paragraph, and even the whole text.

In addition to exact-string searching, concordancers typically permit more sophisticated search patterns, allowing functions such as case-sensitive searches (e.g., to distinguish between "Polish" and "polish"); wildcard searches, in which a special character is used to represent one

```
175 messages that contained the virus before they could be distributed.
t will perform a scan, and if a virus is found, access to the file will
structive tropical storm, macro virus Melissa struck mail servers from
 somewhat different approach to virus protection than other products. T
ut there's a good chance that a virus is the cause. You should stop usi
ttacks these documents. A macro virus conceals itself as a macro in a d
 said. A system that pushes new virus signature files to a subscriber c
essed. Typically, a boot sector virus spreads when an infected diskette
ork administrators in charge of virus protection dealt mostly with tain
 after everyone knows about the virus and how to recognize email messag
1,000 in the past year. A macro virus lodges itself within the document
inually updated with the latest virus signatures. Updates are important
ontrolled. The gateway provides virus protection at the network's most
repared for the latest computer virus set to trigger on Dec. 25. As ano
age that offers more than email virus protection; it can tackle your FT
```

Figure 3.9   A KWIC display of the concordances retrieved for the search pattern "virus."

or more characters in a search string (e.g., "print*" to retrieve "print," "printed," "printer," "printing," "prints," etc., or "dis?s" to retrieve both "discs" and "disks"); and searches using Boolean operators (e.g., AND, OR, NOT) or other regular expressions. Another type of search is a context search, in which another term must appear within a user-specified distance of the search pattern (e.g., contexts in which "printer" appears within five words of "cartridge"). Figure 3.12 shows the results of a wildcard search, while figure 3.13 displays the results of a context search.

Regardless of the type of search pattern entered, the benefit of using concordance lines as a source of linguistic evidence is that they reveal the context in which individual occurrences of words are found. The options for sorting and displaying the data can facilitate the process of observing and distinguishing patterns of linguistic behaviour.

3.2.2.2 Bilingual concordancers

A bilingual concordancer is a tool that can be used to investigate the contents of a parallel corpus. As described in section 3.1.1, a parallel corpus is a corpus that contains a collection of source texts in language

```
t will perform a scan, and if a virus is found, access to the file will
ut there's a good chance that a virus is the cause. You should stop usi
repared for the latest computer virus set to trigger on Dec. 25. As ano
age that offers more than email virus protection; it can tackle your FT
inually updated with the latest virus signatures. Updates are important
ttacks these documents. A macro virus conceals itself as a macro in a d
structive tropical storm, macro virus Melissa struck mail servers from
1,000 in the past year. A macro virus lodges itself within the document
 said. A system that pushes new virus signature files to a subscriber c
ork administrators in charge of virus protection dealt mostly with tain
ontrolled. The gateway provides virus protection at the network's most
essed. Typically, a boot sector virus spreads when an infected diskette
 after everyone knows about the virus and how to recognize email messag
175 messages that contained the virus before they could be distributed.
somewhat different approach to virus protection than other products. T
```

Figure 3.10   A KWIC display of the concordances retrieved for the search pattern "virus" sorted in alphabetical order according to the word immediately preceding "virus."

A aligned with their translations into language B. Alignment is the process whereby sections of the source text are linked up with their corresponding translations. Alignment can take place at many different levels: text, paragraph, sentence, sub-sentence chunk, or even word. Most bilingual concordancers align texts at either the paragraph or the sentence level. Alignments at text level are too high-level to be useful for helping translators find an equivalent for a particular expression, whereas alignment at word level is notoriously difficult and error-prone given the lack of one-to-one correspondence between most natural languages. Some newer bilingual concordancers do, however, employ statistical measures in order to try to identify possible equivalents for specific search terms.

Some programs attempt to do alignment "on the fly" (during the generation of bilingual concordances), but most programs separate the processes of alignment and bilingual concordance generation. For sentence alignment, an automatic alignment tool can be used; however, this is not as trivial a task as one might expect. There are some limitations, and the results depend on the suitability of the texts for alignment. For the best results, the source text and target text must have a

```
after everyone knows about the virus and how to recognize email messag
175 messages that contained the virus before they could be distributed.
ttacks these documents. A macro virus conceals itself as a macro in a d
t will perform a scan, and if a virus is found, access to the file will
ut there's a good chance that a virus is the cause. You should stop usi
1,000 in the past year. A macro virus lodges itself within the document
structive tropical storm, macro virus Melissa struck mail servers from
age that offers more than email virus protection; it can tackle your FT
ork administrators in charge of virus protection dealt mostly with tain
ontrolled. The gateway provides virus protection at the network's most
 somewhat different approach to virus protection than other products. T
repared for the latest computer virus set to trigger on Dec. 25. As ano
 said. A system that pushes new virus signature files to a subscriber c
inually updated with the latest virus signatures. Updates are important
essed. Typically, a boot sector virus spreads when an infected diskette
```

Figure 3.11   A KWIC display of the concordances retrieved for the search pattern "virus" sorted in alphabetical order according to the word immediately following "virus."

similar, if not identical, structure. The most basic level of operation for an automatic alignment tool is to go through the texts sequentially, linking the first sentence of the source text with the first sentence of the target text, then linking the second sentence of the source text with the second sentence of the target text, and so on. One difficulty that may arise is the problem of identifying the end of a sentence. For instance, not all periods represent the end of a sentence (e.g., periods following abbreviations such as Mrs. or Cres., or decimal points in numbers). Other problems include cases in which one sentence in the source text has been translated by two sentences in the target text, or vice versa. These and other difficulties with segmentation and automatic alignment are discussed in greater detail in sections 5.1.1 and 5.2.2.

Like monolingual concordancers, bilingual concordancers retrieve all occurrences of a particular search pattern in its immediate contexts. Most bilingual concordancers are bidirectional, which means that the search pattern can be entered in either language A or language B, regardless of which is the original source language. Some tools also allow bilingual queries in which search terms are entered simultaneously in both languages. Many of the search options available in

```
em to think that any individual virus is going to destroy the world," C
 of detecting and responding to viruses. IBM, for example, by year's en
hardware could be affected by a virus that exerts unusual stress on you
or run an infected program, the virus's code is copied into your PC's m
 e during the process. To combat viruses effectively, you have to arm yo
```

Figure 3.12   A KWIC display of the concordances retrieved using the wild-card search pattern "virus*."

```
machines when an infected floppy disk is left in a drive and the PC is
puter starts up with an infected disk in its drive. Boot-sector viruses
have removed the floppy from the disk drive, proceed to start up the sc
 from the drive. Insert the Scan disk, which will proceed to examine ea
r you have removed the offending disk from the drive, scan the remainin
```

Figure 3.13   A KWIC display of the concordances retrieved using a context search in which "drive" must occur within a five-word span of "disk."

monolingual concordancers (see section 3.2.2.1) are also available in bilingual concordancers (e.g., wildcard searches, context searches). Once retrieved, however, the concordances are usually displayed as paired segments consisting of sentences or paragraphs (depending on the alignment level implemented). The aligned sections are typically displayed either alongside each other, as shown in figure 3.14, or one above the other, as shown in figure 3.15. They can also be sorted in a similar fashion to monolingual concordances (e.g., alphabetically according to the word preceding or following the search pattern).

Because the concordances shown in figures 3.14 and 3.15 have been aligned at paragraph and sentence level, respectively, the program high-lights the search pattern in the search language and retrieves the corresponding target-language segment. It does not highlight the target-language word that corresponds to the search pattern because the alignment is not word-for-word but at the paragraph or sentence level. It is up to the translator to read the corresponding segment and manually identify the precise translation equivalent. Note also that while the search pattern retrieved is always the same, the translation equivalent may vary. For example, as shown in figure 3.15, in the concordances for

Certains objets contiennent des **virus** qui peuvent endommager votre ordinateur. Il est important de s'assurer que cet objet provient d'une source fiable. Êtes-vous sûr que cet objet incorporé provient d'une source fiable?	Some objects contain viruses that can be harmful to your computer. It is important to be certain that this object is from a trustworthy source. Do you trust this embedded object?
ATTENTION : Les pages Web, les fichiers éxécutables ou autres pièces jointes peuvent contenir des **virus** ou endommager votre ordinateur d'une autre façon. Il est important de s'assurer que ce fichier provient d'une source sûre.	WARNING: Web pages, executables, and other attachments may contain viruses or scripts that can be harmful to your computer. It is important to be certain that this file is from a trustworthy source.
Le formulaire de cet élément n'a pas été enregistré dans ce dossier ni dans la bibliothèque de formulaires de votre société. Peut-être préférez-vous ne pas exécuter les macros car cet élément contient des macros susceptibles de contenir un **virus** pouvant endommager votre ordinateur.	The form for this item has not been registered in this folder or in your company's forms library. Because this item contains macros, which could contain a virus harmful to your computer, you may not want to run the macros.

Figure 3.14 Display showing paragraphs aligned side by side, with the search pattern "virus" entered using French as the search language.

Checking for messages to **clean** up off the server...   Vérification des messages à nettoyer depuis le serveur en cours...
Do you want to **clean** up your personalized settings for this program?   Souhaitez-vous supprimer vos paramètres personnalisés pour ce programme?
Unable to **clean** your free/busy information on the server.   Impossible d'effacer les informations de disponibilité sur le serveur.
Cleaner for Downloaded Program Files   Nettoyage des fichiers programmes téléchargés

Figure 3.15 Display showing sentences aligned one above the other, with the wildcard search pattern "clean*" entered using English as the search language.

"clean*," only instances that match the specified search pattern have been retrieved. Instances corresponding to a synonym of "clean," such as "tidy," would not be retrieved. In contrast, however, the translation equivalents do not necessarily follow a uniform pattern. Hence, in the segments that have been retrieved, the translation equivalents for "clean*" include "nettoyer," "supprimer," "effacer," and "nettoyage."

A few bilingual concordancers have attempted to implement more sophisticated features. For instance, some tools try to specifically identify potential equivalents by using statistical measures. For example, if the search term "disk" is entered using English as the search language, the bilingual concordancer retrieves all the sentences in which "disk" occurs, along with the corresponding target sentences. The tool then analyzes the paired segments in an effort to determine which word(s) in the target sentences appear with a frequency similar to that of "disk" in the source segments. The user is then presented with a list of candidates that may be possible equivalents. For example, after analyzing all the paired segments that were retrieved using the search term "disk," the concordancer may propose a list of candidate equivalents that includes the French terms "disque," "disquette," and "lecteur." The user can select one of these candidates and ask to see a KWIC display. In this case, the KWIC concordance for the English segments is displayed in the top half of the screen and the KWIC concordance for the French segments is displayed at the bottom of the screen, as shown in figure 3.16. Segment identifiers (e.g., <S10>, <S17>) can be used to indicate which source-language segments are paired with which target-language segments.

An advantage to this type of search and display is that the source-text and target-text segments can be sorted independently to reveal patterns in both languages. For example, the source-text segments could be sorted alphabetically according to the word that follows the search word, while the target-text segments could be sorted alphabetically according to the word that precedes the search word. As shown in figure 3.17, in the source-language (i.e., English) window, the occurrences of the term "disk" have been sorted alphabetically according to the following word, which reveals patterns such as "disk error" and "disk space." Meanwhile, in the target language (i.e., French) window, the occurrences of the selected equivalent "disque" have been sorted alphabetically according to the preceding word, which reveals the pattern "espace disque." Although the segments in the two windows no longer match chronologically (i.e., the first segment appearing in the

```
<S10>                    The disk is full.
<S17>                     A disk error has occurred during a write oper
<S29>                    The disk is write-protected.
<S33>          Your hard disk may be full or you may not have permis
<S39>      An unexpected disk storage error has occurred.
<S46> r programs, check for disk space on the drive you are saving to a
<S66>                     A disk error occurred and you cannot open thi
<S73>          Make sure the disk is not full or write-protected and tha
<S79> deleted to make more disk space available.
<S94>                    The disk media is not recognized.
<S96>      There is not enough disk space available on your computer to cr
<S98> sure there is enough disk space available on the drive.


<S10>          Le disque est saturé.
<S17>      Une erreur de disque s'est produite lors d'une opération
<S29>          Le disque est protégé en écriture.
<S33>          Votre disque dur est peut-être saturé ou vous n'a
<S39> ndue se rapportant au disque de stockage s'est produite.
<S46>  et vérifiez l'espace disque où vous voulez enregistrer votre fic
<S66> s'est produite sur le disque et vous ne pouvez pas ouvrir ce fich
<S73>      Vérifiez que le disque n'est pas plein ou protégé en écritu
<S79> r libérer de l'espace disque.
<S94>          Le disque support n'est pas reconnu.
<S96>      Espace disque insuffisant pour créer l'index sur v
<S98> urez-vous de l'espace disque du lecteur.
```

Figure 3.16 A bilingual KWIC display in which source- and target-language concordances are displayed in separate windows.

```
<S17>               A disk error has occurred during a write oper
<S66>               A disk error occurred and you cannot open thi
<S10>                   The disk is full.
<S29>                   The disk is write-protected.
<S73>     Make sure the disk is not full or write-protected and tha
<S33>         Your hard disk may be full or you may not have permis
<S94>               The disk media is not recognized.
<S46>   programs, check for disk space on the drive you are saving to a
<S79>e deleted to make more disk space available.
<S96>     There is not enough disk space available on your computer to cr
<S98>   sure there is enough disk space available on the drive.
<S39>     An unexpected disk storage error has occurred.

<S39> ndue se rapportant au disque de stockage s'est produite.
<S17>     Une erreur de disque s'est produite lors d'une opération
<S96>     Espace disque insuffisant pour créer l'index sur v
<S46>   et vérifiez l'espace disque où vous voulez enregistrer votre fi
<S79> r libérer de l'espace disque.
<S98>   urez-vous de l'espace disque du lecteur.
<S10>                   Le disque est saturé.
<S29>                   Le disque est protégé en écriture.
<S66>   s'est produite sur le disque et vous ne pouvez pas ouvrir ce fich
<S73>     Vérifiez que le disque n'est pas plein ou protégé en écritu
<S94>               Le disque support n'est pas reconnu.
<S33>           Votre disque dur est peut-être saturé ou vous n'a
```

Figure 3.17 A bilingual KWIC display in which source- and target-language concordances have been sorted independently.

sorted source-text window is not the translation equivalent of the first segment appearing in the sorted target-language window), users can refer to the segment-identifier numbers to establish which segments belong to the same translation unit.

Another type of bilingual searching offered by some concordancers is a bilingual query in which the user can specify a search term in both languages. In this case, the computer will retrieve and display only the translation units that contain both search terms. For example, if the user executed a bilingual query for the English term "drive" and the French term "lecteur," the computer would retrieve only those paired units in which the term "drive" appeared in the English segment and the term "lecteur" appeared in the French segment, as illustrated in figure 3.18. This type of query is useful for checking whether or not a given translation is attested.

Unlike a monolingual query (a query in which a search term is entered in only one of the two languages), in a bilingual query the concordancer would not retrieve all instances of that individual term. For example, as shown in figure 3.19, the following translation pairs would not be retrieved using the bilingual query "drive"/"lecteur" because both terms are not present.

3.2.3 Collocations

Many corpus-analysis tools also have the ability to compute collocations, which are characteristic co-occurrence patterns of words. Simply put, collocations are generally regarded as words that "go together" or are "found in each other's company." A more technical description is that collocations are words that appear together with a greater than random probability. Because language is not random, certain words tend to cluster together, and some of these clusters form collocations. Collocation generators in corpus-analysis tools typically determine whether two words are collocates by comparing the actual co-occurrence patterns of pairs of words against the patterns that would have been expected if the two words were randomly distributed throughout the text.

One commonly used formula for determining the likelihood that two words are collocates is a mutual information (MI) formula. The MI score between any given pair of words compares the probability that two words appear together as a unit (because they "go together") against the probability that their co-occurrence is simply a result of

The system cannot find the drive specified.	Lecteur introuvable.
Close other programs, check for disk space on the drive you are saving to and on the drive containing your folder, and then save again.	Fermez d'autres programmes et vérifiez l'espace disque où vous voulez enregistrer votre fichier, et le lecteur où se trouve le dossier, puis réenregistrez votre travail.
Make sure there is enough disk space available on the drive that contains your folder.	Assurez-vous de l'espace disque du lecteur contenant le dossier.
Available space on drive: 23MB.	Espace disponible sur le lecteur: 23 Mo.
The drive "Y" is not valid.	Le lecteur « Y » n'est pas valide.
Enter a valid drive letter.	Tapez une lettre de lecteur valide.
The selected disk drive is not in use.	Le lecteur sélectionné n'est pas en service.
The floppy disk in drive A is not formatted.	La disquette dans le lecteur A n'a pas été formatée.
Drive Y does not exist or is not accessible.	Le lecteur Y n'existe pas ou n'est pas accessible.
Make sure you entered the correct drive.	Vérifiez que vous avez tapé le bon nom de lecteur.

Figure 3.18   Concordances retrieved using the bilingual query "drive"/"lecteur."

| Make sure there is enough space available on the hard drive. | Assurez-vous de l'espace du disque dur. |
| The selected optical reader is not in use. | Le lecteur optique sélectionné n'est pas en service. |

Figure 3.19 Concordances that would not be retrieved using the bilingual query "drive"/"lecteur."

Table 3.1   Collocates appearing up to three positions to the left and right of the node "infected"

Collocates of "infected"	3 positions left of node	2 positions left of node	1 position left of node	1 position right of node	2 positions right of node	3 positions right of node
file				26	1	
attachment				11	3	
clean	1	4	7			
document				7	3	
disk				6	1	1
system				5	2	1

chance. For instance, in the sentence "The virus signature has not been recorded," the words "virus" and "signature" occur together because they are part of a multi-word unit. In contrast, in the sentence "The virus that is on my computer is destructive," the words "virus" and "that" occur together, but they do not have any special relationship; their juxtaposition is more a result of chance. If two words are strongly connected, they will have a high MI score. If they have a low level of co-occurrence – if they appear separately more often than together – their MI score will be low (possibly even negative). This means that pairs with high MI scores are more likely to be collocations than words with low MI scores. There are, however, some drawbacks associated with the MI formula. First, it assumes that the different words occur as completely independent events, whereas language is actually full of dependencies (e.g., because of grammatical requirements). Second, MI requires a minimum number of co-occurrences (usually about five) within a corpus in order to be valid.

Once computed, the collocations can be displayed in alphabetical or frequency-ranked order that shows the node word (the search pattern) and the positions to the left and right of the node in which the collocates occur. Collocations do not necessarily appear side by side – sometimes there are one or more intervening words. Many collocation generators can calculate collocates that fall within a user-specified span. For example, as illustrated in table 3.1, in addition to appearing in the position immediately preceding or following the search node, a collocate may appear several places to the left or right.

Table 3.2 provides some examples of patterns in which collocates appear juxtaposed with the node "infected," as well as patterns where

Table 3.2   Sample patterns in which the node "infected" is juxtaposed with collocates or is separated from collocates by one or two intervening words

Node and collocate juxtaposed	Node and collocate separated by one intervening word	Node and collocate separated by two intervening words
infected file	infected backup file	
infected attachment	infected email attachment	
clean infected disks	clean an infected file	clean all the infected diskettes
infected document	infected Word document	
infected disk	infected floppy disk	infected writable optical disk
infected system	infected computer system	infected network operating system

the collocate is separated from the node by one or more intervening words.

3.3 Annotation and mark-up

The corpus processing that has been described so far has been done using "raw" corpora. However, it is possible to encode additional information into a corpus, and this information can be either linguistic or non-linguistic in nature. The addition of linguistic information is usually referred to as annotation, while the addition of non-linguistic information is typically known as marking up a corpus. The decision about whether or not a corpus should be annotated and/or marked up depends on the project at hand, and, like the issue of corpus design, that of corpus annotation/mark up falls largely outside the scope of this book. Nevertheless, it will be touched on briefly here because it can involve the use of automated tools, such as taggers.

One popular type of linguistic annotation is known as syntactic annotation, in which each word in the corpus has its associated part of speech specified with tags. Unfortunately, there is no single standard tag set: each tagger uses its own set of tags. As shown in table 3.3, some taggers use very general part-of-speech notations (e.g., "verb," "noun"), while others use more specific notations (e.g., "imperative verb," "plural common noun"). Note that even punctuation marks get tags.

It would take a very long time to add all the parts of speech to a corpus manually, but there are programs called taggers that can do this automatically. Many taggers claim upward of 95 percent accuracy,

Table 3.3   Two examples of part-of-speech tagging for the sentence "Scan for viruses regularly"

	Tagged sentence	Tag set	
Part-of-speech annotation using general tags	Scan<VB> for<PREP> viruses<NN> regularly<ADV> .<PUNC>	VB PREP NN ADV PUNC	= verb = preposition = noun = adverb = punctuation mark
Part-of-speech annotation using more specific tags	Scan<VB0> for<II> viruses<NN2> regularly<RR> .<YSTP>	VB0 II NN2 RR YSTP	= imperative verb = general preposition = plural common noun = adverb = full stop

which is reasonable for many purposes. However, for sentences containing 14 or more words, the level of accuracy is typically less than 50 percent. If a higher degree of accuracy is desired, the output will need to be checked and edited by a human.

Another type of linguistic annotation, known as semantic annotation, can be used to distinguish between the multiple meanings of a word. Homonyms are words that look the same but have different meanings when used in different contexts. For instance, "bank" can be used to refer to 1) a financial institution or 2) the side of a river. Semantic annotation (e.g., bank1 vs bank2) could be used to distinguish between the different senses of a word.

The advantage of having a linguistically annotated corpus is that it allows users to focus their searches more narrowly. For example, a translator may wish to retrieve all instances of the word "test" where it appears as a verb but not as a noun, or all instances of the word "bank" when it appears in sense 1 but not in sense 2. Such retrieval patterns would not be possible in an unannotated corpus, from which all occurrences that match the string "test" (whether noun or verb), or "bank" (whether sense 1 or sense 2), would be retrieved.

A way of adding non-linguistic information to a corpus could be to mark up different structural sections of the texts (e.g., title, subtitle, sentence, paragraph, section, chapter). In this way, it would be possible to ask the computer to retrieve only occurrences of a specific search pattern that appear, for instance, in the title of a text. Other non-linguistic information that could be added to a corpus includes publication date, text type, subject field, author- or translator-related details, and so on; however, such information would need to be added manually.

The advantage of a "raw" corpus is that it is easier and faster to build. Annotating or marking up a corpus requires a greater initial investment of time, but subsequently allows more specific searching. Consequently, there is a trade-off between the time required to anno-tate/mark up and the benefits gained by doing so. For example, if a corpus is going to be used for only one small translation project, it may not be worth annotating it. In addition, a translator may find that in a small corpus, it is faster to manually separate out the desired contexts (e.g., "test" the verb) from the undesired ones (e.g., "test" the noun) than it would be to automatically annotate and then proofread the cor-pus. This raises another general point to keep in mind: the more auto-matic processing that is done to a text (e.g., scanning, aligning, tagging), the greater the chance of introducing errors along the way that may later need to be manually detected and corrected.

3.4 Benefits and drawbacks of working with corpus-analysis tools

Corpus-analysis tools have been in use for some time by language pro-fessionals such as foreign-language teachers and lexicographers, and translators are becoming increasingly aware of the advantages offered by such tools. As always, however, the advantages must be carefully weighed against the drawbacks before a decision is made about whether using a tool will be truly beneficial in any given situation.

3.4.1 Frequency data

Frequency data are not easily obtainable from resources such as dictio-naries or printed parallel texts, but word-frequency lists can be easily generated using corpus-analysis tools. Such lists are simple yet power-ful. In a translation context, they can help translators to determine which words seem to be "important" in the corpus on the basis of fre-quency, and translators can compare the frequencies of different words. For example, a translator can use a frequency list to help deter-mine whether a term appears to be commonly used by experts in the subject field or appears to be the idiosyncratic preference of a small group of users. Similarly, when faced with a choice of two or more syn-onyms, the translator can consult a frequency list to see which of the terms is more commonly used. Of course, frequency alone is not always sufficient for determining whether a given term is appropriate, but the data generated by the frequency list can be further investigated using other features of corpus-analysis tools such as concordancers and collocation generators.

3.4.2 Context

One of the greatest advantages of corpus-analysis tools is that they allow translators to see terms in a variety of contexts simultaneously, which, in turn, allows them to detect various kinds of linguistic and conceptual patterns that are sometimes difficult to spot in isolated printed resources. It is important to emphasize once again, however, that although the corpus-analysis tools present information in a manner that makes it easier to analyze, they do not actually do any analysis; it is up to the translator to interpret the data.

3.4.3 Availability and copyright

As well as interpreting data, the translator must provide them. Corpus-analysis tools are not typically accompanied by corpora; in any case, it is up to the translator to compile a corpus that is suitable for the project at hand. Depending on the languages, subject field, and text type in question, it may be reasonably easy or relatively difficult to compile a corpus.

In the case of monolingual corpora, there is a considerable amount of information available in English on a wide variety of subjects and in a broad range of text types. However, if a translator is working with a less widely used language and in a very specialized subject field, it may be more difficult to find texts to put into a corpus. As the Internet increases in popularity and as access to such technology spreads around the globe, this situation will gradually improve.

With regard to bilingual parallel corpora, availability may also be an issue. There are currently very few pre-constructed corpora of this type available, so translators will likely have to compile their own corpora in the relevant subject field and language pair. This means identifying existing translations and aligning the texts as described in section 3.2.2.2. However, as the popularity of tools such as translation memories (see chapter 5) begins to increase, it will become easier to either construct or gain access to bilingual parallel corpora.

Another important consideration when building a corpus is whether or not a text can legally or ethically be included in a corpus. Like printed texts, electronic texts are subject to copyright laws, and if a user wishes to hold a text in a corpus, it is first necessary to establish the precise details of the text's ownership and obtain the owner's permission. Because the Internet is such a new phenomenon, copyright laws in many countries predate this technology, which means that they are sometimes unclear about ownership of electronic texts. Nevertheless, many countries are in the process of updating their laws to address this issue, and translators would be wise to investigate the ownership of any text and obtain permission before including it in a corpus. If the corpus is strictly for personal use, it may be acceptable to include a text (or a portion of a text) in it without obtaining permission, in the same way that it is legal to produce photocopies of documents (or parts of documents) for personal use; however, if the corpus is going to be used for commercial purposes, it is absolutely essential to obtain copyright permission.

3.4.4 Pre-processing

As discussed in section 2.3, different software applications work with different file formats, so the files in the corpus must be converted to the format that is used by the corpus-analysis tool in question. Many corpus-analysis tools process plain text (ASCII) files, which do not require much effort in the way of pre-processing, although unwanted line or paragraph breaks may need to be deleted. Furthermore, the ASCII character set is limited and therefore some accented letters or foreign characters may not be represented. Other tools may require the corpus to be converted into a special format. In addition, we have already discussed other types of pre-processing that may be required, for example, converting printed text into electronic form using OCR or voice-recognition technology (see sections 2.1 and 2.2), annotating or marking up a corpus (see section 3.3), and aligning text in the case of bilingual parallel corpora (see section 3.2.2.2). The greater the amount of pre-processing that needs to be done, the more time the translator will have to devote to carrying out this processing and verifying that it has been done correctly (proofreading and editing).

3.4.5 Speed and information-retrieval issues

Once a corpus has been compiled, one advantage is that translators can typically work more quickly with electronic media than with printed media. This means that they can consult a greater number of documents and that the consultation process can be much faster, as corpus-analysis tools enable users to focus their research by allowing them to access relevant document sections directly, rather than requiring them to read the documents in a linear fashion from beginning to end.

Nevertheless, translators must develop sensible search strategies for consulting corpora. Corpus-analysis tools are not intelligent – they work using pattern matching techniques. Therefore, they will retrieve exactly what users ask them to retrieve, even if this is not necessarily what the users want to retrieve. Common problems include "silence" and "noise." In the case of silence, a pattern that is of interest to the user is not retrieved because the search string is not comprehensive enough. For example, a translator may be interested in examining all contexts that contain any form of the verb "to go." The wildcard search pattern "go*" will retrieve most forms of the verb "to go," including "go," "goes," "going," and "gone," but it will not retrieve the simple past form "went." Likewise, a search pattern that is too broad will retrieve noise (patterns that are not of interest). For example, if a translator wants to examine all contexts that contain a form of the verb "to enter," he or she might try using the wildcard search pattern "enter*." This will retrieve forms such as "enter," "entered," "entering," and "enters," but it will also retrieve all forms of "entertain," "enterprise," and even "enterogastritis" if these terms happen to appear anywhere in the corpus. In order to reduce both noise and silence, translators must think carefully about the search strategies they use. It may even be necessary to develop different search techniques for working with different languages or subject fields.

Other potential retrieval problems include homographs and homonyms. As mentioned in section 3.2.1.1, homographs are words that have the same spelling but have different parts of speech; for example, "cooks" can be a noun ("Too many *cooks* spoil the broth") or a verb ("He *cooks* dinner for his mother every Wednesday"). In contrast, homonyms are words that have the same spelling and the same part of speech, but have different meanings; for instance, "ball" can be a noun that refers to a round object used in sports (e.g., "golf ball," "tennis ball") or a noun that refers to a large formal gathering for social dancing (e.g., "masquerade ball," "debutante ball"). If a user is working with an unannotated corpus, there will be no way for the computer to distinguish between homographs and homonyms, and so the data may be slightly distorted. If it is important for users to be able to automatically distinguish between words having different senses or parts of speech, it will be necessary to annotate the corpus accordingly (see section 3.3).

Finally, multi-word units may be difficult to identify when using a feature such as a word-frequency list. Word-frequency lists generally treat white space as a boundary between words, but some coherent concepts can be expressed only using a multi-word unit (e.g., "operating system," "boot sector virus"). It will not be possible to identify or determine the frequency of multi-word units using word frequency lists, although other features such as concordancers or collocation generators may be useful for helping to identify and count these units. Alternatively, another type of software, known as term-extraction software, may prove useful for identifying them (see section 4.4).

3.4.6 Character sets and language-related difficulties

Some technical difficulties may arise for translators working with certain languages. Not all corpus-analysis tools come equipped with the character sets for all languages. While many Indo-European languages can be processed without difficulty, some tools may not be able to handle languages that are not based on the Roman alphabet, such as Arabic, Greek, Hebrew, and Russian.

Asian languages, such as Chinese, Japanese, and Korean, present further difficulties. Whereas the characters of many languages can be stored using one byte (one unit of storage), Asian languages with complex characters require two bytes to store a single character. Such a language is therefore said to have a double-byte character set (DBCS). Unfortunately, many computer applications, including many corpus-analysis tools, have been written in such a way that they can process only single-byte characters. Therefore, translators who work with double-byte languages may not be able to use certain corpus-analysis tools. Fortunately, a double-byte method for encoding all characters, known as Unicode, is now emerging as an industry standard (Unicode Consortium, 2000), and it is hoped that applications developers will incorporate double-byte encoding into all future products and releases.

Another problem that may arise for some languages is alignment. In order to create a bilingual parallel corpus, the alignment tool must be able to divide the source text into segments (e.g., sentences, paragraphs). This means that the system must be able to recognize which elements indicate the end of a segment (e.g., punctuation). When working with languages that do not use Indo-European-style punctuation, alignment tools may have difficulty determining where one segment ends and the next begins, which means it is therefore difficult to align the corresponding segments of the source and target texts.

3.4.7 Economic aspects

For the most part, corpus-analysis tools are very reasonably priced, many costing less than a few hundred dollars, which is within the budget of many translators. In addition, they do not typically have excessive hardware requirements, though as corpora grow in size, translators will require sufficient disk space to store them on. A number of corpus-analysis tools are described in Appendix B.

KEY POINTS

- A corpus is a large collection of electronic texts that have been gathered according to specific criteria to meet the needs of a particular project.
- There are a number of different types of corpora, including monolingual corpora, monolingual comparable corpora, aligned bilingual parallel corpora, and non-aligned bilingual comparable corpora.
- Corpora can be "raw" (simply containing text) or annotated/ marked up (having additional information – such as part-of-speech tags or structural divisions – encoded into the text).
- Corpus-analysis tools allow users to access, manipulate, and display the information contained within a corpus in a variety of useful ways.
- Key features offered by most corpus-analysis tools include word-frequency lists, concordancers, and collocation generators.
- Word-frequency lists allow users to discover how many different words there are in a corpus and how often each appears.
- Concordancers retrieve all occurrences of a particular search pattern in its immediate contexts and display these in an easy-to-read format (e.g., KWIC).
- Collocations are generally regarded as words that "go together," and collocation generators typically determine whether two words are collocates by comparing the actual co-occurrence patterns of pairs of

words against the patterns that would have been expected if the two words were randomly distributed throughout the text.

- It is very important to note that corpus analysis tools do not interpret the data – it is still the responsibility of the translator to analyze the information found in the corpus.

FURTHER READING

- Engwall (1994), Bowker (1996), Meyer and Mackintosh (1996), Pearson (1998), Austermühl (2001), and Bowker and Pearson (2002) discuss issues relating to corpus design and compilation.
- Barnbrook (1996), Kennedy (1998), McEnery and Wilson (1996), and Bowker and Pearson (2002) provide good introductions to corpus linguistics tools and techniques.
- Bowker (1998, 2000), Lindquist (1999), and Bowker and Pearson (2002) investigate how corpora can be exploited as translation resources.
- L'Homme (1999a, chapter 6) and Bowker and Pearson (2002) explain how monolingual and bilingual concordancers work and explore how they can be useful to translators.
- Pearson (1996) and Zanettin (1998) explore how corpus analysis tools can be integrated into the translation classroom.
- Garside, Leech, and McEnery (1997) provide information on various types of corpus annotation.

4. Terminology-Management Systems

... users who try to use standard spreadsheet, database, or word-processing programs to manage terminological data almost inevitably run into problems involving compromised data integrity due to inadequate modeling features, in addition to difficulties manipulating large volumes of data as resources grow over time.

Schmitz (2001, 539)

A major part of any translation project is identifying equivalents for specialized terms. Subject fields such as computing, manufacturing, law, and medicine all have significant amounts of field-specific terminology. In addition, many clients will have preferred in-house terminology. Researching the specific terms needed to complete any given translation is a time-consuming task, and translators do not want to have to repeat all this work each time they begin a new translation. A terminology-management system (TMS) can help with various aspects of the translator's terminology-related tasks, including the storage, retrieval, and updating of term records. A TMS can help to ensure greater consistency in the use of terminology, which not only makes documentation easier to read and understand, but also prevents miscommunications. Effective terminology management can help to cut costs, improve linguistic quality, and reduce turnaround times for translation, which is very important in this age of intense time-to-market pressures.

TMSs have been in existence for some time. Early efforts to use computers for terminology management began in the 1960s and eventually led to the development of several large-scale term banks, such as

Eurodicautom, Termium, and the Banque de terminologie du Québec (now known as the Grand dictionnaire terminologique), which were maintained on mainframe computers by large organizations. In the 1980s, when desktop computers became available, personal TMSs were among the first CAT tools commercially available to translators. Although they were very welcome at the time, these early TMSs had some limitations. They were designed to run on a single computer and could not easily be shared. They typically allowed only simple management of bilingual terminology and imposed considerable restrictions on the type and number of data fields as well as on the maximum amount of data that could be stored in these fields. Recently, however, this type of software has become more powerful and flexible, particularly in terms of storage and retrieval options.

4.1 Storage

The most fundamental function of a TMS is that it acts as a repository for consolidating and storing terminological information for use in future translation projects. Previously, many TMSs stored information in structured text files, mapping source-to-target terminology using a unidirectional one-to-one correspondence. This caused difficulties, for example, if a French-English term base needed to be used for an English-French translation. The newer, more sophisticated software stores the information using a relational model. This means that the information is stored in a more onomasiological or concept-based way, which permits mapping in multiple language directions.

There is also increased flexibility in the type and amount of information that can be stored on a term record. Formerly, users were required to choose from a predefined set of fields (e.g., subject field, definition, context, source), which had to be filled in on each term record. The number of fields was often fixed, as was the number of characters that could be stored in each field. For instance, if a TMS allowed for only one context, the user was forced to record only one context, even though it may have been useful to provide several. An example of a typical conventional record template is provided in figure 4.1.

In contrast, as illustrated in figure 4.2, most contemporary TMSs have adopted a free entry structure, which allows users to define their own fields of information, including repeatable fields (e.g., for multiple contexts) and some even permit the inclusion of graphics. Not only can users choose their own information fields, they can also arrange

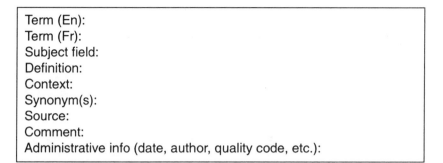

Figure 4.1   TMS term record with a fixed set of predefined fields.

and format them, choosing different layouts, fonts, or colours for easy identification of important information. This means that the software can be adapted to suit a specific user's needs and can grow as future requirements change. The amount of information that can be stored in any given field or record has also increased dramatically. Different term bases can be created and maintained for different subject fields or clients, and some systems allow multiple term bases to be merged if desired.

4.2 Retrieval

Once the terminology has been stored, translators need to be able to retrieve this information. A range of search and retrieval mechanisms is available. The simplest search technique consists of a look-up to retrieve an exact match. Some TMSs permit the use of wildcards for truncated searches. A wildcard is a character, such as an asterisk, that can be used to represent any other character or string of characters. For instance, a wildcard search using the search string "comput*" could be used to retrieve the term records for "computer," "computing," and so on. More sophisticated TMSs also employ fuzzy matching techniques. A fuzzy match will retrieve term records that are similar to the requested search pattern, but that do not match it exactly. Fuzzy matching allows translators to retrieve records for morphological vari-ants (e.g., different forms of verbs, words with suffixes or prefixes), spelling variants (or even spelling errors), and multi-word terms, even if the translator does not know precisely how the elements of the

Term (En):   **select** (v)
Subject field: computing
Context 1:   *The item you selected does not exist.*
    Source: Computer magazine ABC, 1999
Context 2:   *When you are finished selecting the text, click on the Format menu.*
    Source: User manual XYZ, 1998

Client: Company A
Fr: **sélectionner**
Date: June 2000

Client: Company B
Fr: **choisir**
Date: January 2001

Figure 4.2   TMS term record with free entry structure.

Table 4.1   Sample term records retrieved using fuzzy matching

Search pattern entered by user	Term record retrieved using fuzzy matching
"anovulatory"	ovulation
"discs"	disk
"department for dangerous goods emergencies"	Dangerous Goods Emergency Centre

Table 4.2   Sample hit lists retrieved for different search patterns

Hit list containing records that match the wildcard search pattern "*cake"	Hit list containing records that match the fuzzy search pattern "skate-boarding champion"
cheesecake	champion
cupcake	skateboard (n)
fruitcake	skateboard (v)
pancake	skateboarding
	International Skateboarding Championships

multi-word term are ordered. Table 4.1 provides some examples of the term records that could be retrieved using fuzzy matching techniques.

When wildcard searching or fuzzy matching is used, it is possible that more than one record will be retrieved as a potential match. When this happens, users are presented with a "hit list" of all the records in the term base that may be of interest, and they can select the record(s) that they wish to view. Sample hit lists are shown in table 4.2.

4.3 Active terminology recognition and pre-translation

Another feature offered by some TMSs, particularly those that operate as part of an integrated package with word processors and translation-memory systems (see section 5.5.9.1) is known as active terminology recognition. This feature is essentially a type of automatic dictionary look-up. As the translator moves through the text, the terminology-recognition component compares items in the source text against the contents of the term base, and if a match is found, the term record in question is displayed for the user to consult.

Some TMSs also permit a more automated extension of this feature in which a translator can ask the system to do a sort of pre-translation or

Table 4.3   Automatic replacement of source-text terms with translation equivalents found in a term base

Source text sentence	Term base entries for items contained in the source text	Sentence produced following pre-translation
The file operation cannot be completed because the disk is full.	disk – *disque* file operation – *opération de fichier* full – *saturé*	The *opération de fichier* cannot be completed because the *disque* is *saturé*.

batch processing of the text. In this case, the TMS will identify terms for which an entry exists in the term base, and it will then automatically insert the corresponding equivalents into the target text. The result of this pre-translation phase is a sort of hybrid text, as shown in table 4.3. In a post-editing phase, it is up to the translator to verify the correctness of the proposed terms and to translate the remainder of the text for which no equivalents were found in the term base.

4.4 Term extraction

Another feature that may be included in some TMSs is a term-extraction tool, which is sometimes referred to as a term-recognition or term-identification tool. Most term-extraction tools are monolingual, and they attempt to analyze source texts in order to identify candidate terms. However, some bilingual tools are being developed that analyze existing source texts along with their translations in an attempt to identify potential terms and their equivalents. This process can help a translator build a term base more quickly; however, although the initial extraction attempt is performed by a computer, the resulting list of candidates must be verified by a human, and therefore the process is best described as being computer-aided or semi-automatic rather than fully automatic.

Unlike the word-frequency lists described in section 3.2.1, term-extraction tools attempt to identify multi-word units. There are two main approaches to term extraction: linguistic and statistical. For clarity, these approaches will be explained in separate sections; however, aspects of both approaches can be combined in a single term-extraction tool.

Antivirus programs now include a number of options. Integrity checking performs checks of the status of the files against the information that is stored in a database. Behaviour blocking performs before-the-fact detection. Heuristic analysis is a form of after-the-fact detection.

Figure 4.3   A short text that has been processed using a linguistic approach to term extraction.

Antivirus programs now include more options. Integrity checking performs periodic checks of the current status of the files against the stored information. Behaviour blocking performs before-the-fact detection. Heuristic analysis is a form of after-the-fact detection.

Figure 4.4   A slightly modified version of the text that has been processed using a linguistic approach to term extraction.

4.4.1 Linguistic approach

Term-extraction tools that use a linguistic approach typically attempt to identify word combinations that match particular part-of-speech patterns. For example, in English, many terms consist of NOUN+ NOUN or ADJECTIVE+NOUN combinations. In order to implement such an approach, each word in the text must first be tagged with its appropriate part of speech, as described in section 3.3. Once the text has been correctly tagged, the term-extraction tool simply identifies all the occurrences that match the specified part-of-speech patterns. For instance, a tool that has been programmed to identify NOUN+NOUN and ADJECTIVE+NOUN combinations as potential terms would identify all lexical combinations matching those patterns from a given text, as illustrated in figure 4.3.

Unfortunately, not all texts can be processed this neatly. If the text is modified slightly, as illustrated in figure 4.4, problems such as "noise" and "silence" become apparent.

First, not all of the combinations that follow the specified patterns will qualify as terms. Of the NOUN+NOUN and ADJECTIVE+NOUN candidates that were identified in figure 4.4, some qualify as terms ("antivirus programs," "integrity checking," "behaviour blocking," "heuristic analysis"), whereas others do not ("more options," "periodic checks," "current status," "stored information"). The latter set constitutes noise and would need to be eliminated from the list of candidates by a human.

Another potential problem is that some legitimate terms may be formed according to patterns that have not been pre-programmed into the tool. This can result in "silence" – a situation in which relevant information is not retrieved. For example, the terms "before-the-fact detection" and "after-the-fact detection" have been formed using the pattern PREPOSITION+ARTICLE+NOUN+NOUN; however, this pattern is not common and is not likely to be recognized by many term extraction tools.

A final drawback to the linguistic approach is that it is heavily language dependent. Term-formation patterns differ from language to language. For instance, term-formation patterns that are typical in English (e.g., ADJECTIVE+NOUN, NOUN+NOUN) are not the same as term-formation patterns that are common in French (e.g., NOUN+ADJEC-TIVE, NOUN+PREPOSITION+NOUN). Consequently, term-extraction tools that use a linguistic approach are generally designed to work in a single language (or closely related languages) and cannot easily be extended to work with other languages.

4.4.2 Statistical approach

The most straightforward statistical approach to term extraction is for a tool to look for repeated series of lexical items. The frequency threshold (the number of times that a series of items must be repeated) can often be specified by the user. For example, as illustrated in figure 4.5, if the minimum frequency threshold is set at two, a given series of lexical items must appear at least twice in the text in order to be recognized as a candidate term by the term-extraction tool.

Based on a minimum-frequency threshold of two, the text in figure 4.5 yielded two potential terms: "antivirus software" and "virus signature files." Unfortunately, this simple strategy often leads to problems because language is full of repetition, but not all repeated series of lexical items qualify as terms. For instance, consider the slightly modified version of the text shown in figure 4.6.

Working solely on the basis of identifying repeated series of lexical items, the term-extraction software has identified two additional can-

Major <u>antivirus software</u> developers are introducing automated updating of <u>virus signature files</u> and <u>antivirus software</u>. Updates will soon be available as often as once an hour, via the Internet. Some developers update their <u>virus signature files</u> up to six times a day. A number of developers now offer the convenience of push-technology updating, which only requires a one-time setup to guarantee continuously up-to-date <u>virus signature files</u>.

Figure 4.5   A short text that has been processed by a statistical term-extraction tool using a minimum frequency threshold of two.

Major <u>antivirus software</u> <u>developers are</u> introducing automated updating of <u>virus signature files</u> and <u>antivirus software</u>. Updates will soon be available <u>as often as</u> once an hour, via the Internet. Some <u>developers are</u> updating their <u>virus signature files</u> <u>as often as</u> six times a day. A number of <u>developers are</u> now offering the convenience of push-technology updating, which only requires a one-time setup to guarantee continuously up-to-date <u>virus signature files</u>.

Figure 4.6   A slightly modified version of the text that has been processed by a statistical term-extraction tool using a minimum frequency threshold of two.

didates: "developers are" and "as often as." These candidates constitute "noise" rather than terms, and they would need to be eliminated from the list of potential terms by a human. Stop lists, as described in section 3.2.1.2, can be used to reduce the number of unlikely terms that may otherwise be identified as candidates. For instance, a stop list could be implemented to instruct the term-extraction tool to ignore series that begin or end with function words, such as prepositions, articles, and conjunctions.

Another drawback to the statistical approach is that not all of the terms that appear in a given text will be repeated, which may lead to "silence." For instance, in figure 4.6, the term "push-technology updating" was not identified as a candidate because it only appeared once in the text and the minimum frequency threshold was set to two.

A related statistical approach to identifying candidate terms is to calculate mutual information (MI), as described in section 3.2.3. The premise here is that if two lexical items appear together more often than they appear separately, the multi-word unit in question may be a potential term. Once again, however, this approach is not foolproof, and noise and silence may occur.

Nevertheless, the use of statistics as a basis for term extraction does have one clear strength: it is not language dependent. This means that a statistical term-extraction tool can, in principle, be used to process texts in multiple languages.

4.5 Additional features

TMSs may also include other types of utilities, such as features that allow users to create and manage concept systems or thesauri, merge multiple term bases, import from or export to other formats, or print out the contents of a term base in a user-specified glossary format.

4.6 Benefits and drawbacks of working with a TMS

The idea behind maintaining a glossary of any kind is that it encourages terminological consistency and saves translators from having to repeat their research each time they start a new translation project. It is not necessary to use specialized software to maintain a glossary – many translators have long been using card indexes or word processors to create terminology records. Terminology-management software does offer a number of advantages over these conventional approaches, but modern technologies are not without their shortcomings. The benefits and drawbacks of working with TMSs are outlined below.

4.6.1 Speed and flexibility

The principal advantages of using terminology management software rather than a card index have largely been outlined in sections 4.1 and 4.2: TMSs permit more flexible storage and retrieval. In addition, it is easier to update electronic information, and faster to search through electronic files. Even though a word processor allows information to be stored in electronic form, it is not an adequate tool for managing terminology in an efficient way, and its search facilities slow down considerably as the term base grows in size. Another way that a TMS can potentially speed up a translator's work is by allowing terms to be pasted directly into the target text, thus avoiding the need to retype the term. Of course, terms may need to be edited to fit into the context (e.g., a verb may need to be conjugated), which means that time saved on copying and pasting may need to be spent on editing. In some cases, this has led to a new way of recording information on terminology records, and this is discussed in section 4.6.3.

4.6.2 Quality

Although any type of glossary can help to improve consistency throughout a translation project, the active terminology-recognition feature of some TMSs takes this one step further. As Clark (1994, 306) notes, there is little point in going to the trouble of ensuring that terminology is agreed to beforehand and stored in a term base if translators choose not to consult this term base. With active terminology recognition, the choice is taken out of their hands because terms in the source text are automatically checked against the term base.

4.6.3 Changing the nature of the task

In addition to speeding up the task of searching for terminology, there is some evidence that the technology is beginning to have an impact on the amount and type of terminological information that is being recorded on a term record, as well as on the way in which this information is being recorded.

Although flexible tools do allow users to enter detailed information into glossaries, it is becoming increasingly common to see glossaries used in the localization industry that contain only the source and target term, and perhaps a comment if the source term has multiple possible translations depending on the context. According to O'Brien (1998, 118), there are several reasons for this type of stripped-down glossary format. First, the required turnaround time in the localization industry is often so short that it does not allow for the preparation of detailed glossaries. Second, the terminology used (even by the same client) can change rapidly, warranting new glossaries each time the client has a product localized. Finally, the translator, who also has to produce very fast turnaround times, is interested only in the client-approved translated term and the context in which a term can occur if there is more than one translation for that term. Of course, this trend has been caused more by the nature of the translation market than by the nature of the technology itself; however, the fact that technology makes it easy to compile and transfer information quickly has contributed to the trend of treating glossaries as disposable items, rather than as long-standing records.

The technology is, however, responsible for prompting a change in both the type of data that are being stored and the way in which they are recorded on term records. For example, in integrated packages (packages that are linked with other applications, such as word processors or translation memories), translators can automatically insert terminology from the TMS directly into the target text (e.g., by clicking on the term in the term record). This can save time, as there is no need to retype or cut and paste. One result of this is that some translators are creating term records for phrases or expressions that occur frequently in a specialized subject field but do not qualify as terms in the conventional sense. For instance, a translator working on the translation of a computer manual may create term records for expressions such as "click on OK" or "it's easy to" because it is faster to insert these frequently used expressions directly from the TMS than it is to type them.

Of course when terminology is inserted into the target text from the TMS, some editing may be required (e.g., to conjugate a verb), and this has raised an interesting question regarding which form of a term should be recorded on a term file. Traditionally, term files have always contained the canonical form of a term (the singular form of a noun, the infinitive form of a verb, the masculine form of an adjective) (Dubuc 1985, 80; Rondeau 1984, 84). However, Kenny (1999, 71) has observed that in order to reduce the amount of time spent editing terms that have been inserted directly from TMSs, some translators are now choosing to record the most common form of a term, or indeed several forms of a term, in the term record, as shown in figure 4.7. This way, the correct form can be inserted simply by clicking on it, and there will be no need to edit the term in the target text. Further discussion on the integration of TMSs and translation memory systems can be found in section 5.5.9.1.

4.6.4 Shareability of information: networking, file formats, and standards

Terminology-management systems can be used as stand-alone tools, but more and more, they are being networked so that several users can access and contribute to the term base. In such cases, it may be desir-

```
En:  select
     selected
     selecting
     selects

Fr:  sélectionner
     sélectionne
     sélectionnez
     sélectionné
     sélectionnée
     sélectionnées
     sélectionnés
```

Figure 4.7   A sample term record in which multiple forms of the term have been recorded.

able to give different users different types of privileges on the network system. For instance, all users should be able to consult the information stored in the term base, but only some users, such as translators responsible for quality control, should be able to add new records.

Another way of sharing terminological information is by exchanging data with clients or with other translators. Unfortunately, not everyone uses the same TMS. As explained in section 2.3, different applications store information in different formats, so in order to exchange information the file formats must be either compatible or convertible. Some TMSs will allow data to be exported directly to various word-processor or desktop-publishing formats or to be imported and exported according to international standards, such as the Machine-Readable Terminology Interchange Format (MARTIF – ISO 12200). A new standard, known as Term Base eXchange (TBX), is currently under development by the Open Standards for Container/Content Allowing Reuse (OSCAR) special-interest group belonging to the Localization Industry Standards Association (LISA).

4.6.5 Character sets and language-related difficulties

A limitation of some TMSs is the character sets that can be handled. As explained in section 3.4.6, many computer applications, including some TMSs, have been written in such a way that they can only process single-byte characters. Therefore, translators who work with languages that require double-byte character sets (e.g., Chinese, Japanese, Korean) may not be able to use certain TMSs. This problem is now being addressed by numerous developers, who are seeking to incorporate double-byte encoding into future products and releases by adopting the Unicode Standard.

4.6.6 Economic aspects

Most translators will not find the cost involved in acquiring and maintaining a TMS to be prohibitive. Many systems are reasonably priced and can run on basic desktop computers that have limited memory and processing power. The amount of storage space required will depend on the size of the term base(s). However, if a translator wishes to run the TMS as part of an integrated suite with a translation memory system (see section 5.5.9.1), the system requirements and price will go up. Details on some commercially available products are located in Appendix B.

KEY POINTS

- Terminology-management software has existed in one form or another since the 1960s, but contemporary software features a number of improvements, including more powerful and flexible storage and retrieval options.
- Contemporary TMSs store information in a concept-oriented fashion, which permits mapping in multiple language directions.
- They can also store more information and have a free entry structure, which allows users to define and format their own data fields.
- Retrieval features include wildcard searches, fuzzy matching, active terminology recognition, pre-translation and term extraction.
- TMSs can be networked to facilitate the sharing of data, and standards have been developed to allow data exchange between different systems.
- There is evidence to indicate that this technology is bringing about some changes in conventional terminographic practice (e.g., the forms that are recorded on term records).

- Austermühl (2001, chapter 7) compares the advantages and disadvantages of maintaining term records using file cards, word processors, spreadsheets, databases, hypermedia systems, and TMSs.
- Rondeau (1984, chapter 6) and Sager (1990, chapter 6) provide a historical overview of term banks.
- Schmitz (1996) provides a good overview of TMSs, while Lauriston (1997) and Schmitz (2001) outline criteria for evaluating TMSs.
- Wright (2001) describes the evolution of entry structures and TMS design.
- Jaekel (2000) and Warburton (2001) present case studies that describe how a TMS has been successfully implemented in a company.
- Melby (1998) and Melby, Schmitz and Wright (2001) discuss terminology-exchange formats.
- O'Brien (1998) and Kenny (1999) explore some ways in which technology has brought about changes in conventional terminographical practice.
- Kageura and Umino (1996), Lauriston (1997), L'Homme (1999a, chapter 8), Ahmad and Rogers (2001), and Cabré, Estopà and Vivaldi (2001) discuss term-extraction tools. Gaussier (2001) focuses specifically on bilingual term-extraction tools.

5. Translation-Memory Systems

One of the most important sources of information to which a translator can have access is a large body of previous translations.

Kay and Röscheisen (1993, 122)

Given the staggering volume of translations produced year after year, it is quite obvious that existing translations contain more solutions to more translation problems than any other available resource.

Isabelle (1993, 8)

The concept of a translation memory (TM) has existed for some time. Melby (1995, 187) notes that the idea originated in the 1970s, and the first implementations came about in the 1980s, but only since the late 1990s has this type of tool developed into a significant commercial entity. Many of the tools that are commercially available today were first developed as in-house tools used by translation bureaus to support client work, but as TMs have become more widely available, their popularity with other professional translators has grown steadily.

A TM is a type of linguistic database that is used to store source texts and their translations. The texts are broken down into short segments that often correspond to sentences (see section 5.1.1). As shown in figure 5.1, a translation unit is made up of a source text segment and its translated equivalent. Most simply, a TM can be viewed as a list of source-text segments explicitly aligned with their target-text counterparts. The resulting structure is sometimes referred to as a parallel corpus or a bitext (see section 3.1.1).

These translation units are stored in the TM database. Some sophisti-

Translation unit 1	EN: The following document name has invalid characters or is too long. FR: Le nom du document ci-dessous est trop long ou contient des caractères non valides.
Translation unit 2	EN: Please rename the document. FR: Veuillez renommer le document.

Figure 5.1   Display of translation units.

cated TM programs use a type of technology called a neural network to store information. A neural network allows information to be retrieved more quickly than a sequential search technique.

The essential idea behind a TM system is that it allows a translator to reuse or "recycle" previously translated segments. Reusing a previous translation in a new text is sometimes referred to as "leveraging." Although language is dynamic, it is quite repetitive, and people often use the same or similar expressions when communicating similar ideas. The volume of translation is increasing, and most translators have had the experience of being asked to translate a text containing passages that they (or their colleagues) have translated on a previous occasion. In the past, many people did not keep archives of previous translations, and those who did often collected them in an unsystematic way or in a form that could not be searched easily (e.g., on paper). Even when electronic copies have been kept, it may prove difficult and time consuming to locate the necessary segment. For example, if a translator kept copies of previous translations in word-processor files, he or she would likely need to undertake a multi-step approach along the following lines in order to be able to reuse a previous translation.

- Locate the appropriate source-text file (which often entails deciphering a cryptic filename).
- Open the source-text file and use the word processor's search feature to locate the appropriate segment.
- Open the target file (the translation).

- Scroll down through the target file to the approximate location of the target segment.
- Begin reading to locate the appropriate target equivalent.
- Copy and paste the desired target segment into the new translation.
- Edit the segment accordingly.

In many cases, translators taking this approach may end up spending so much time opening various files, searching, copying and pasting, and editing that it would have been faster to retranslate the segments from scratch.

In recent years, researchers and developers have been working hard to find a solution to this problem, and one result of their efforts has been TM systems – a new type of CAT tool that allows translators to reuse, and thereby profit from, the great volume of previously translated work.

5.1 How does a TM system work?

This technology works by automatically comparing a new source text against a database of texts that have already been translated. When a translator has a new segment to translate, the TM system consults the database to see if this new segment corresponds to a previously translated segment. If a matching segment is found, the TM system presents the translator with the previous translation, as shown in figure 5.2. The translator can consult this previous translation and decide whether or not to incorporate it into the new translation.

5.1.1 Segmentation

In most instances, the basic unit of segmentation in a TM system is the sentence, and this explains why TMs are sometimes known as sentence memories. However, not all text is written in sentence form. Headings, list items, and table cells are familiar elements of text, but they may not strictly qualify as sentences. Therefore, many TM systems allow the user to define other units of segmentation in addition to sentences. These units can include sentence fragments or even entire paragraphs.

Deciding what constitutes a segment is not as trivial a task as it might appear to be. At first glance, it seems reasonable to decide that full sentences will qualify as segments, but how can the TM system identify sentences? Punctuation marks such as periods, exclamation

New source segment	The filename is not a valid name.
Stored TM unit	EN: The filename is not a valid name.
	FR: Le nom de fichier n'est pas valide.

Figure 5.2 A new source text segment and the matching translation unit stored in the TM.

points, and question marks are typically used to indicate the end of a sentence, but already problems are beginning to arise. What happens in the case of abbreviations, such as Mr., Dr., St., U.S.A., i.e., and etc.? The periods that follow abbreviations do not always indicate the end of a sentence, nor do the periods that are found in decimal numbers or in numbered section headings. The ellipsis is another form of punctuation that can appear either in the middle or at the end of a sentence. An additional difficulty is the case of embedded sentences, such as the following: "When you see the message 'Do you wish to continue?' click on OK." Colons and semi-colons are punctuation marks that users may or may not wish to include as end-of-segment markers. In the case of languages that do not use Indo-European-style punctuation, there are additional difficulties (see section 5.5.5).

Some of these problems can be resolved by incorporating stop lists (e.g., lists of abbreviations that do not indicate the end of a sentence, such as Mrs. and e.g.) into the TM system. Other segmentation decisions, such as whether or not a colon is used to represent the end of a segment, may be left up to the user.

An additional segmentation-related issue is the fact that the segmentation units used in the source text may not correspond exactly to those used in the translation. For example, it is possible for one source-language sentence to be split into two target-language sentences, or vice versa. This lack of one-to-one correspondence can create difficulties for automatic alignment programs, and such problems will be further explored in section 5.2.2. Table 5.1 provides examples of some different types of segmentation.

5.1.2 Matches

Most TM systems present the user with a number of different types of

Table 5.1   Some different types of segmentation

Heading	EN: Warning:
	FR: Avertissement :
One sentence translated by one sentence	EN: This computer program is protected by copyright law and international treaties.
	FR: Ce logiciel est protégé par les lois et les traités internationaux sur le droit d'auteur.
One sentence translated by two sentences	EN: Unauthorized reproduction or distribution of this program, or any portion of it, may result in severe civil and criminal penalties, and will be prosecuted to the maximum extent possible under the law.
	FR: Toute reproduction ou distribution partielle ou totale, par quelque moyen que ce soit, est strictement interdite. Toute personne ne respectant pas ces dispositions se rendra coupable du délit de contrefaçon et sera passible des sanctions pénales prévues par la loi.
Two sentences translated by one sentence	EN: The "0" button and the "1" option affect the current application. The other options affect all applications.
	FR: Les modifications apportées par le bouton « 0 » et l'option « 1 » n'affecteront que l'application en cours alors que les autres options seront répercutées dans toutes les applications.

segment matches. The most common types are exact, fuzzy, and term matches. Some TM developers are now working on new types of matches, such as full and sub-segment matches, but these features have not yet been implemented in many systems. Furthermore, the existing matching techniques used in many TM systems have some limitations.

5.1.2.1 Exact matches

The most straightforward matches are known as exact or perfect matches. An exact match is 100 percent identical to the segment that the translator is currently translating, both linguistically and in terms of formatting. The process used by a TM system to identify perfectly matching segments is one of strict pattern matching. This means that the two strings must be identical in every way, including spelling, punctuation, inflection, numbers, and even formatting (e.g., italics,

Table 5.2 Examples of segments that will not be retrieved as exact matches

Different spelling	Change the color of the font. Change the colour of the font.
Different punctuation	Open the file and select the text. Open the file; and select the text.
Different inflection	Delete the document. Delete the documents.
Different numbers	Use version 1.1. Use version 1.2.
Different formatting	Click on OK. Click on OK.

bold). Any segment in the new source text that does not match an original segment precisely will not produce an exact match, as shown in table 5.2.

It is important to remember that even when the TM system retrieves what appears to be an exact match, the translator is not forced to accept the proposed translation. Indeed, there are times when the proposed translation may not be appropriate, such as when a client has expressed a preference for using a particular style or term. Even though a segment may be identical, translators are concerned with translating complete texts rather than isolated segments, so it is important to read the proposed translation in its new context to be certain that it is both stylistically appropriate and semantically correct. For example, in cases where homonymy arises, a segment could in fact be an accurate translation when considered in isolation, but not if placed in the wrong context. Homonyms are words that look the same but have two (or more) different meanings. For instance, the English word "pipe" can refer to a cylindrical conduit used to transport a substance such as water or natural gas, or it can refer to a device for smoking. Depending on the intended meaning, the word could be translated into French as either "tuyau" (conduit) or "pipe" (smoking). In a TM system that treats segments as isolated units, the segments shown in table 5.3 would be presented as an exact match.

However, in a text about plumbing, it is unlikely that this would be the appropriate translation. The translator must take care to read the proposed segment in the larger context and edit the suggested translation if necessary to be sure that the correct meaning is being conveyed.

Table 5.3   Example of an exact match retrieved from a TM

New source segment	Empty the pipe.
Stored TM unit	EN: Empty the pipe.
	FR: Videz la pipe.

5.1.2.2 Full matches

As mentioned in section 5.1.2, some TM system developers have introduced a new type of match, known as a full match, into their systems.
A full match occurs when a new source segment differs from a stored
TM unit only in terms of so-called variable elements, which are sometimes referred to as "placeables" or "named entities." Variable elements include numbers, dates, times, currencies, measurements, and
sometimes proper names. These elements typically require some kind
of special treatment in a text. For example, most personal or company
names are not usually translated, while dates or times may have their
format changed (e.g., DD/MM/YY may become MM/DD/YYYY or 2
PM may become 14:00). In any case, the precise number or proper name
that appears in the source-text segment does not generally affect how
the rest of the segment is translated. However, in a TM system that
uses superficial character matching as a way of identifying potential
translation equivalents, the presence of a different date or proper noun
may result in a potentially useful match being overlooked, as illustrated in table 5.4.

In the example shown in table 5.4, the segment stored in TM unit 2
would provide a translator with more useful information than would
the segment stored in TM unit 1; however, because proper names,
dates, and times have been included in the character-matching process,
TM unit 1 has been identified by the system as a better match than TM
unit 2. To improve their usefulness, TM systems need to ignore variable elements for matching purposes, and some systems are already
beginning to integrate such strategies.

5.1.2.3 Fuzzy matches

Of course, not every passage that a translator encounters will have
been expressed in exactly the same way in a previous text or will differ
from a previous text solely in terms of variable elements. Nevertheless,

Table 5.4   Examples from a TM that uses character matching

	Character matches	Comments
New source segment	The party for John is scheduled for 03-30-00 at 4pm.	The new source segment has a total of 52 characters.
Stored TM unit 1	EN: The game with John is scheduled for 03-30-00 at 4pm.	This segment would be retrieved as the best match because it differs from the new source segment by only 8 characters.
	FR: Le match contre John est prévu le 30 mars 2000 à 16h.	
Stored TM unit 2	EN: The party for Mary is scheduled for 28/11/99 at 16:00.	This segment would not be identified as the best match because it differs from the new source segment by 17 characters.
	FR: La fête pour Mary est prévue le 28 novembre 1999 à 16h.	

passages that are similar may still be of some use, and for this reason, many TM systems are capable of locating fuzzy matches, sometimes known as approximate or partial matches. A fuzzy match retrieves a segment that is similar, but not identical, to the new source segment. A good TM system will highlight the differences between the segments in order to draw the translator's attention to areas that may need to be edited before the proposed translation can be integrated into the new target text. Some systems use colour coding to illustrate various types of differences between the new source text segment and the retrieved segment. Figure 5.3 contains an example of a fuzzy match.

The degree of similarity in a fuzzy match can range from 1 percent to 99 percent, and the user generally has the ability to set the sensitivity threshold to allow the TM system to locate previously translated segments that may differ only slightly from the new source text segment or segments that vary greatly. If the sensitivity threshold is set too high (e.g., a minimum of 95 percent similarity), there is a risk that the TM system will produce "silence": potentially useful partial matches will not be retrieved. However, if the sensitivity threshold is set too low (e.g., a minimum of 10 percent similarity), there is a risk that the TM system will produce "noise": the suggested translations that are retrieved will be too different from the new source-text segment and

New source segment	The specified file is not valid.
Stored TM unit	EN: The specified file is not a valid file. FR: Le fichier spécifié n'est pas un fichier valide.

Figure 5.3   A fuzzy match retrieved from a TM.

New source segment	The text for the property of the command is either missing a right parenthesis or includes a misplaced left parenthesis.
Stored TM unit	EN: The text for the property of the command is missing a right square bracket or includes a misplaced left square bracket. FR: Le texte de la propriété de la commande ne se termine pas par un crochet, ou le crochet ouvrant est mal placé dans le texte.

Figure 5.4   A TM segment retrieved using a high sensitivity threshold.

therefore will not be helpful. When the threshold is very low, a match may be made on the basis of very general words (e.g., "the," "and," "of," "to") and the overall content of the retrieved segment may contain little of value for helping the translator to translate the new segment. Figures 5.4 and 5.5 contain examples of segments retrieved using high and low sensitivity thresholds. Many translators prefer to set the sensitivity threshold somewhere between 60 and 70 percent; however, depending on the nature of the text in question, some translators have found that matches with a similarity as low as 40 percent can still provide helpful information (O'Brien 1998, 117). Although fuzzy matching can be useful, it requires careful proofreading and editing to ensure that the proposed translation is appropriate for inclusion in the new target text.

New source segment	The specified operation failed because it requires the file to be active.
Stored TM unit	EN: The specified language for the file is not supported on this computer. FR: La langue spécifiée pour le fichier n'est pas prise en charge par cet ordinateur.

Figure 5.5   Example of a TM segment retrieved using a low sensitivity threshold.

As shown in figure 5.6, some TM systems will retrieve more than one fuzzy match from the TM (provided that all of these matches fall within the bounds of the user-specified sensitivity threshold). In such cases, the entire range of matches is presented to the translator in an order that ranks them from best (the segment that most closely resembles the new source text segment) to worst (the segment that is the most different from the new source text segment). The translator can view all the retrieved matches and determine which, if any, can best be adapted for use in the new translation.

5.1.2.4 Term matches

Most TM systems operate in conjunction with an associated term base (see chapter 4 and section 5.5.9.1). Using compatible terminology-management software, a translator can build up a bilingual term base, and the TM system will compare the individual terms contained in each source text segment against the terms contained in the term base. This process is known as active terminology recognition, and it essentially constitutes automatic dictionary lookup (see section 4.3). For example, as shown in table 5.5, if one or more terms are recognized as being in the term base, the TM system points to the appropriate term records and the translator can then make use of the relevant information contained there. This means that when no exact or fuzzy matches are found for source-text segments, the translator might at least find some translation equivalents for individual terms in the term base.

New source segment	The operation was interrupted because the file was hidden.
Stored TM unit (best match)	EN: The operation was interrupted because the Ctrl-c key was pressed. FR: L'opération a été interrompue car la touche Ctrl-c a été enfoncée.
Stored TM unit (second-best match)	EN: The specified method failed because the file is hidden. FR: La méthode spécifiée a échoué car le fichier est masqué.
Stored TM unit (third-best match)	EN: The operation was interrupted by the application. FR: L'opération a été interrompue par l'application.
Stored TM unit (fourth-best match)	EN: The requested operation cannot be completed because the disk is full. FR: Le disque est saturé. Impossible de continuer l'opération requise.

Figure 5.6   Multiple fuzzy matches retrieved and ranked.

Table 5.5   Term matches retrieved by a TM system working in conjunction with a term
base

New source segment	There may not be enough <u>memory</u> available on your <u>computer</u>.
Term base entry	EN: memory FR: mémoire (f)
Term base entry	EN: computer FR: ordinateur (m)

5.1.2.5 Sub-segment matches

As mentioned above, some TM system developers are now attempting
to implement a new type of matching, which operates at the sub-
segment level. Sub-segment matching falls partway between fuzzy
and term matching. As described in section 5.1.2.3, in fuzzy matching,
the TM system compares the entire new source segment against complete segments stored in the TM database, and the two segments must
have a number of elements in common in order for a match to be established. The higher the sensitivity threshold, the more similar two segments must be overall in order for a fuzzy match to be established.

In term matching, as outlined in section 5.1.2.4, the new source segment is compared against entries in a term base. This term base has been
compiled separately by the translator, and can be integrated with the
TM system in order to take advantage of active terminology recognition.

How then does sub-segment matching differ from fuzzy matching
and term matching? At first glance, it might appear that sub-segment
matching is simply fuzzy matching with a very low sensitivity threshold; however, in the case of fuzzy matching, the similarity is deter-
mined based on the overall similarity of the two segments, as shown in
figure 5.7.

In the case of sub-segment matching, the elements that are compared
are smaller chunks of segments. This means that a match can be
retrieved between two small chunks of segments, even if the complete
segments do not have a high degree of overall similarity. For example,
the two segments shown in figure 5.8 would not likely be retrieved as
part of a fuzzy match, because when taken as a whole, the segments
are not very similar: one segment is considerably longer than the other;
one ends with a semi-colon and the other with a period; one has formatting (boldface); one is part of a numbered list; and so on. Neverthe-

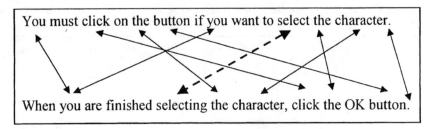

Figure 5.7   A fuzzy match based on overall similarity.

New source segment	First, <u>check for disk space on the drive</u> that contains the **Temp** folder;
Stored TM unit	EN: 3. Close other programs, <u>check for disk space on the drive</u> you are saving to, and then save again. FR: 3. Fermez des applications, vérifiez l'espace disque disponible sur le lecteur où vous voulez enregistrer votre fichier, puis réenregistrez votre travail.

Figure 5.8   A sub-segment match.

less, both of these segments contain a chunk that is very similar indeed, and there is a possibility that the translator may be able to reuse that chunk.

A sub-segment match also differs from a term match. Although it is technically possible to store arbitrary strings of words in a term record, translators have traditionally restricted term-record entries to lexical items that are used to refer to specific concepts in a specialized subject field. Therefore, while a term base might conceivably contain entries for terms such as "disk space" or "drive," it would be unlikely to contain an entry for the sub-segment chunk "check for disk space on the drive," as seen in the example in figure 5.8. (However, as noted in section 4.6.3, some translators are now beginning to store frequently used strings in their term bases even when these strings do not constitute "terms" in the conventional sense.)

New source segment	The file operation cannot be completed because the disk is full.
Sub-segment match	EN: There is not enough memory to perform the file operation. FR: Mémoire insuffisante pour continuer cette opération de fichier.
Sub-segment match	EN: This action cannot be completed because the program is busy. FR: Impossible de continuer cette action car le program est occupé.
Sub-segment match	EN: Disk is full. FR: Le disque est saturé.

Figure 5.9   Different sub-segment matches can be combined to provide a translator with helpful suggestions.

As a further refinement, some TM system developers are working on a combined full-segment/sub-segment approach that will allow the TM system to automatically compare the new source-text segment against the stored TM using several iterations. It will begin by examining complete segments, first looking for exact matches and then for fuzzy matches, and if no such match is found at the segment level, it will compare increasingly smaller chunks in an effort to find a match. In this way, as shown in figure 5.9, the translator may be presented with sub-segment matches originating from several different segments, even if none of those complete segments qualified as a fuzzy match.

This strategy is similar to the approach used in example-based machine translation (EBMT). The principal difference between a TM as a support tool for translators and a full-fledged EBMT system is basically a question of who has the primary responsibility for doing the translation. With a TM, the translator is responsible for analysis of the segments and formulation of the target text, whereas with EBMT, the computer is responsible for producing a complete draft of a target text, though this may still need to be post-edited by a human translator.

5.1.2.6 No matches

Because no two texts are the same, there will likely be segments for which no useful match is retrieved. In such cases, the new source segment must be translated by the translator from scratch, although it is possible that equivalents for some of the terms may be located in an associated term base (see section 4.3). Another option is to use a machine-translation system to translate the portions of the source text for which no match was found in the TM (see section 5.5.9.3). Regardless of which method is used, once a source-text segment has been translated, it can then be added to the TM so that it will be available for reuse in the future.

5.1.2.7 Limitations of existing matching algorithms

Although the various matching techniques outlined above are useful in many situations, they do have some limitations. A serious limitation of many current TM systems is their inability to deal with inflection and derivation (Macklovitch and Russell 2000).

Inflection is the process that is used to make a noun plural (e.g., "boy" + "s" = "boys") or to conjugate a verb (e.g., "talk" + "ed" = "talked"). In order to identify potential matches, some TM systems use very superficial methods such as comparing the overall similarity of the characters in the new and stored segments. In such cases, inflection may distort the similarity and thus prevent a potentially useful match from being retrieved, as illustrated in table 5.6.

From the translator's point of view, the segment contained in TM unit 2 is actually more similar to the new source segment than is the segment contained in TM unit 1, and it would therefore be more helpful for producing an accurate translation. The differences between the new source segment and the segment in TM unit 2 are simply differences of inflection – the nouns have been pluralized and the verb has been conjugated in the past tense and made to agree with the plural subject. A translator could easily make the relevant inflectional adjustments in the new source text. In contrast, although the new source segment and the segment stored in TM unit 1 are quite similar on a superficial level (in terms of the total similarity of the individual characters), they are very different in terms of their meaning. In this case, the differences are not merely a result of inflection; rather, they are completely different lexical items that have very different translations

Table 5.6.   Examples of shortcomings in TM systems

	Character matches	Comments
New source segment	The pattern on the dish is very appealing.	The new source segment has a total of 42 characters.
Stored TM unit 1	EN: The pattern on the disk is very revealing. FR: Les tendances statistiques qui se trouvent sur la disquette sont très révélateurs.	This segment would be retrieved as the best match because it also has 42 characters and differs from the new source segment by only 4 characters.
Stored TM unit 2	EN: The patterns on the dishes were very appealing. FR: Les motifs sur la vaisselle étaient très agréables.	This segment would not be identified as the best match because it has 47 characters and differs from the new source segment by 7 characters.

and would therefore be of limited use in helping the translator deal with the new source-text segment.One step toward improving TM systems would be to enable them to recognize and match variants of a word (i.e., so that "dish" would match "dishes" but not "disk"). The underlying assumption here is that for a user who wishes to find translations for a sentence containing a given word X, the translations of any sentence containing an inflectional variant of X (such as Xes or Xing,) could be potentially informative, regardless of the minor adjustments that would need to be made to accommodate the inflectional variation. A similar approach could be used to deal with derivation, which is the process of adding a prefix or suffix to an existing word in order to create a new one (e.g., the addition of the suffix "ly" to the adjective "cautious" produces the adverb "cautiously") (Macklovitch and Russell 2000, 142).

5.2 Creating a TM

A TM system is essentially a type of database. In other words, it is a piece of software that allows a user to store and retrieve information. Recent advances in database technology and computer power have made it possible for TM systems to store and quickly retrieve large amounts of previously translated material. However, as is the case with any database system, the information must be provided by the user. Therefore, when a translator first purchases a TM system, the database is empty. It is not until the translator begins to store some data (source and target texts) in the TM system that it becomes useful. Indeed, the greater the number of texts stored in the database, the greater the likelihood that some type of match will be found. Nevertheless, size should not come at the expense of organization. It is not necessary, and may not be desirable, to build only one TM. Translators may find it more useful to create separate TMs for different subject fields (e.g., in order to reduce false hits caused by homonymy), or to have different TMs for different clients (e.g., to accommodate terminological and stylistic preferences). Keep in mind that a larger TM will result in a greater number of matches only if the texts in it contain vocabulary and structures similar to those found in the new source text. Therefore, while it may seem logical at first glance to build a single large TM covering all subject fields or clients, this may actually turn out to be a false economy because only a percentage of the texts in the TM are likely to provide good matches. Moreover, there is a greater likelihood of retrieving "noise" (e.g., matches that are not helpful, matches containing homonyms) and the translator may waste a considerable amount of time analyzing, eliminating, or editing these poor matches.

There are two main ways in which translations can be entered into the TM database: through interactive translation or through post-translation alignment. As we will see, the strength of one method is the weakness of the other: interactive translation has the potential to produce a TM that is high in quality but (initially) low in volume, whereas post-translation alignment has the potential to produce a TM that is higher in volume but (possibly) lower in quality. Of course, the two methods are not mutually exclusive, and it is entirely possible to build a TM using a combination of both.

5.2.1 Interactive translation

The most straightforward way of constructing a TM is for translators to carry out the translation work within the TM environment, adding translation units to the memory as they go along. Each time the translator translates a source-text segment, the paired translation unit (the source text segment and its equivalent translation) can be stored in the

TM database. Once a segment has been translated and stored, it immediately becomes part of the TM. This means that if that segment (or a similar one) occurs again in the text – even in the very next sentence – the previous translation is suggested to the translator automatically. As explained above, the translator then has the choice of accepting the previous translation or editing it if the context requires change.

Creating a TM through interactive translation generally results in a higher-quality database; however, depending on the volume of work that a translator produces, or on the number of translators contributing, it can take a considerable amount of time to build a TM of any significant size using this approach. It is worth pointing out, however, that many TM systems can be networked, which means that multiple translators can contribute to one TM, and the volume of data that it contains can be built more quickly. In a networked situation, it is also possible to give different types of privileges to different users in order to exercise some form of quality control. For example, all users can be given permission to consult the TM, but the ability to add new translation units can be restricted to revisers or senior translators. Translation units produced by junior translators can be sent to a "holding tank" where they can be verified by a reviser before being stored in the TM.

A drawback of the interactive approach to constructing a TM is that translators are not able to reuse any of the translation work they did before they acquired a TM system. Therefore, another way of entering information into a TM is through post-translation alignment.

5.2.2 Post-translation alignment

Most TM systems also contain a feature for aligning existing translations, which will potentially allow translators to reuse translations from their archives (provided these texts are in electronic form). Alignment is the process of comparing a source text and its translation, matching the corresponding segments, and binding them together as translation units in a TM. As mentioned in section 3.2.2.2, a few systems attempt to do alignment "on the fly" (when a search is in progress); however, most systems require alignment to be carried out prior to searching. An automatic alignment tool can be used for this process; however, as we saw with segmentation (section 5.1.1), this is not as trivial a task as one might expect. There are some limitations, and the results depend on the suitability of the texts for alignment. For the best results, the source and target texts must have a similar, if not identical, structure.

Table 5.7.   Sample translation units in which the French translations are longer than the English source segments

---

EN: The file path is invalid.
FR: Le chemin d'accès au fichier est non valide.

EN: Unable to write preferences to registry.
FR: Impossible d'enregistrer les préférences dans la table de registres.

EN: A disk error has occurred during a seek operation.
FR: Une erreur de disque s'est produite lors d'une opération de recherche.

One technique for automatic alignment includes exploiting the natural correlation between the lengths of translated segments. For instance, looking at the sample translation units in table 5.7, the French translations appear to be approximately 35 percent longer than their corresponding English source segments.

Based on these sample sentences, an automatic alignment program might therefore anticipate that all French translations would be somewhere between 25 and 45 percent longer than their corresponding English source segments. If during the alignment process the program encountered a situation in which the French segment appeared to be 75 percent longer than the English segment, or in which the English segment appeared to be longer than the French segment, the program would alert the user and ask for help. As discussed in section 5.1.1, such situations might arise in cases in which two source-language segments have been translated by a single target-language segment, or vice versa.

Other automatic alignment techniques involve making use of cognate word pairs or known translations. In such cases, translation equivalents in a bilingual machine-readable lexicon can be used as anchor words to help link source and target segments. Therefore, if a given word appears in the source segment, the alignment program expects to find its listed equivalent in the corresponding target segment. Other types of clues that can be similarly used to guide the alignment process include numbers, acronyms, and formatting (e.g., bold, italics, underlining). If any of these features are found in a source-text segment, the alignment program expects to find them in the corresponding target-text segment.

Such techniques are not typically able to cope with situations such as inversion, in which sentences or paragraphs may be presented in a different order in the target text than they were in the source text. Another type of alignment problem occurs when a section of the target text has not been translated (e.g., a culture-specific reference may have been dropped), or when a new section has been added to the target text that did not appear in the source text (e.g., an explanation of a source-text reference). In automatic alignment, it is almost inevitable that some segments will be misaligned. There are ways of dealing with this, such as sending misaligned sentences to a separate file to be excluded from the TM or to be manually aligned by a human. Of course, some misalignments may slip through, so it is important for a translator to verify that the automatic alignment has been done accurately and to manually correct errors, if necessary, in order to maintain a standard of quality. TMs that have been created by interactive translation are typically more accurate than those that have been created by automatic alignment, but alignment can produce a reasonably accurate TM that can be used as a starting point. This may be important, especially for translators working alone or in small companies, because, as previously mentioned, it can take a considerable amount of time for an individual to build a TM using the interactive-translation approach. The principal benefit of a TM is that it allows translators to reuse previous translations; however, in order to do this, the TM must actually contain previous translations, and the greater the volume of text in the TM, the greater the chance that identical or similar segments will be found for reuse in new translations. Post-translation alignment allows translators to "bulk up" their TMs and thereby increase the probability of getting a match. One type of reuse that post-translation alignment does not allow for, however, is the reuse of internal repetitions (see section 5.4.1).

5.3 Working with an existing TM

Once information has been entered into the TM database, either through interactive translation or by post-translation alignment, the translator has a TM available for use when undertaking new translations. There are two main methods of working with an existing TM: interactive mode and batch mode.

5.3.1 Interactive mode

A translator working in interactive mode follows the same process as described in section 5.2.1 for building a TM through interactive translation. As the translator proceeds to work through the new source text segment by segment, the TM system attempts to match the segments stored in the database against the new source-text segments. If a match is found, the system presents the previous translation to the translator, who has the choice of accepting, modifying, or rejecting this proposal. As each new segment is translated, the translation unit is immediately added to the TM and is available for reuse the next time an identical or similar segment is encountered. In this way, the TM is being built as the translator works.

5.3.2 Batch mode

Most TM systems also allow for batch translation, sometimes referred to as pre-translation, which means that a user can run a complete source text through the system and, whenever it finds an exact match, it will automatically replace the new source-text segment with the translation that is stored in the TM. Segments for which no match is found must later be translated by either a human translator (see section 5.1.2.6) or a machine-translation system (see section 5.5.9.3). In either case, the entire text must then be post-edited by a human translator to ensure that the replacements made by the system were correct. If the translator makes changes to any matches that were inserted automatically, these changes can subsequently be added to the TM to keep it up to date.

5.4 Texts that are suitable for use with a TM

Not all texts are equally suitable for inclusion in a TM. Given that the aim of a TM is to allow translators to reuse previously translated work, it makes sense that the types of texts that are best suited for working with a TM are those that are repetitive or that will be updated or revised. Texts that are written about highly specialized subjects are also good candidates for inclusion in a TM, particularly if the translator using the TM frequently works in that subject field. The characteristics of different texts that can most usefully be translated with the help of a TM are described below.

5.4.1 Texts containing internal repetitions

One type of text that is conducive for use with a TM is a text that contains a great deal of repetitive content, which is referred to as a text with internal repetitions. The higher the percentage of repetitive content, the more desirable it is to use a TM system. From the moment a segment is stored in the TM, it becomes available for reuse – it can even be used to help translate the very next segment of the new source text! The process of reusing an internal repetition is sometimes referred to as propagation.

There are many different genres of texts, but some tend to contain more repetition than others. Typically, technical, scientific, and legal texts tend to contain repetition, whereas literature and advertising texts tend to contain less repetition and are therefore typically less suitable for inclusion in a TM.

5.4.2 Revisions

Revisions are another type of text that can be successfully translated with the help of a TM. A revision is an amended version of a previous text. Frequently, user manuals fall into this category. Imagine that a manual for a given product has been written and translated. The following year, some new features are added to the product and the descriptions corresponding to these new features are added to the manual. As a result, the revised manual may differ from the original manual by only 20 percent. Now imagine that the translator who was commissioned to do the translation of the original manual had stored that work in a TM. Instead of retranslating the entire manual, the translator can reuse the previous translations for the parts of the manual that have not been altered (in this example, 80 percent of the text) and can then concentrate on translating the new additions that have been made (20 percent of the text).

Web pages are another example of texts that are frequently revised. Commercial Web sites are revised on a regular basis, which can be monthly, weekly, or even daily.

5.4.3 Recycled texts

Some translators work in specialized fields where the subject matter and format of the texts that they translate does not vary greatly. Some translators also work regularly for the same client, who may have terminological and stylistic preferences. In such cases, even though a new source text may not be an actual revision of a previous text, there may be similar passages in other texts (these are sometimes referred to as external repetitions) that can successfully be recycled into the new source text. As mentioned previously, the reuse of these external repetitions is sometimes referred to as leveraging.

5.4.4 Updates

Another type of text that can be usefully translated with the help of a TM is an update. Updates occur when the client makes changes to the source text while the translation is still in progress. Receiving an update can cause serious difficulties for a translator, particularly if the text is long and changes have been made throughout the document. Without a TM, the translator would have to physically compare the original and the updated source texts looking for changes (e.g., with the help of a "track changes" feature in a word processor). In contrast, with a TM system, the translator can run the updated source text through the system and it will quickly identify new or changed segments.

Using a TM in this way means that a translator can begin the translation process even before the source text is finalized. As noted in section 1, as more companies begin selling products on the global market, there is increasing pressure to release their products simultaneously around the world. This means that product documentation must be available simultaneously in many languages. If a translator does not receive a source text until it has been finalized, that translator will likely have a very tight deadline for producing the translation. However, if the translator receives drafts of the original document in the early stages of development, the text can be translated and stored in the TM database. Then, as updated sections of the source text are made available, the translator can run the updates through the TM in order to isolate the new or modified parts from those that have already been translated.

5.5 Benefits and drawbacks of working with a TM

Advances in computer storage capacity and processing speed mean that translators can now have fast and efficient access to large textual databases of previous translations; however, as well as bringing such benefits, technology also has limitations. Like most forms of technology, TM systems have their supporters and their critics. Obviously, each translator and client will have his or her own opinion about the usefulness of such tools, and the following section merely aims to out-line a number of the perceived benefits and drawbacks of this approach to translation.

First, however, it must be emphasized that TM system performance is dependent on the scope and quality of the existing database and is expected to improve as the database grows. A TM is of no use if it is empty, and the quality of the translations stored in the TM is depen-dent on the skill of the translator. Remember that a TM is a CAT tool that is designed to support translators, but the translations suggested by the TM are in fact texts that have been previously translated and stored in the database by a human translator. Moreover, source texts and their translations must be explicitly stored in the TM. Any transla-tion work performed outside the TM environment will not automati-cally be stored in the database and will therefore not be available for reuse in the future, unless, of course, it is aligned and added at a later stage (see section 5.2.2).

5.5.1 Time

One of the most widely professed advantages of a TM is that it saves time. Translators who are able to reuse portions of a previous transla-tion will be able to translate texts more quickly, and by increasing their productivity, they will, in principle, be able to earn more money. At first glance, this argument seems convincing; however, it may be over-simplifying the issue somewhat.

Whenever a new way of working is introduced, there will be a learn-ing curve. In the case of TMs, translators must learn to master a new and fairly sophisticated software application, which requires them to draw upon skills that are unrelated to the craft of translation. In some cases, translators may need to learn several packages since their vari-ous clients may use different TM systems. Although learning to use such software is becoming an essential part of the job, it may take a translator several weeks to feel comfortable working with a new soft-ware package. There will more than likely be some stress involved, as the need to learn a new package will inevitably coincide with an important deadline! Therefore, translators may actually see an initial drop in productivity during this learning phase, although productivity will begin to increase as they become habituated to the software. Fur-thermore, as previously mentioned, the larger the TM, the greater the likelihood of getting a match and being able to reuse previous translations. When a translator first begins working with a TM, it will likely be rather small and there will be few matches, but the system's performance will improve as the TM grows. It is important for translators not to become frustrated and give up on TMs too soon, because significant gains in productivity are likely to be in the middle to long term rather than the short term.

The importance of identifying a suitable sensitivity threshold for fuzzy matching has been discussed in section 5.1.2.3, but it is worth repeating here. On the one hand, if the threshold is set too high, fuzzy matches that could potentially be helpful may not be retrieved. On the other hand, if the threshold is set too low, the matches retrieved may not be very useful. Some translators feel that editing a fuzzy match may actually take longer than translating a segment from scratch. Other translators feel that even if the fuzzy matches cannot be incorporated directly into the new translation, they may provide useful clues, inspiration, or direction to additional research.

Finally, it should be pointed out that converting files to and from the required TM format requires additional steps that may prove to be time-consuming (see section 5.5.4).

5.5.2 Quality

As previously mentioned, a TM is a CAT tool and not a machine-translation tool. The translations stored in the TM are provided by a human translator; therefore, a prerequisite for obtaining a high-quality result from a TM is that the translations stored there by humans must be correct in the first place. If the contents of the TM are of poor quality, the users must spend time correcting the translations, and they risk losing any time that they may have saved by working with the TM in the first place. Furthermore, it is important to note that even though translations may be accurate when they are initially stored in a TM, they may become inaccurate over time (e.g., if terminology changes) or they may be inappropriate in a given context (e.g., if they contain homonyms or if they are client-specific). Similarly, since last-minute changes are often made to a translated text after it has been reconverted to its original format, the changes are not always inserted into the TM, which means it is difficult to keep the TM up to date. As a result, quality control must be treated as an ongoing process, and it is not advisable for translators to reuse previous translations without first verifying that they are correct. This can lead to a conflict between the promise of increased productivity (as described in section 5.5.1) and the need to maintain high quality. There is a fear that some translators who are working on tight deadlines might find it tempting to work too quickly when using TMs, blindly substituting proposed translations without verifying their accuracy.

If one assumes that the contents of the TM are correct, an oft-cited benefit of working with a TM system is that it improves consistency. A translator who is working on a long document is able to maintain consistency throughout the text. This is particularly helpful when a translator receives an update (see section 5.4.4) in which changes may have been made throughout the document. In addition, many TM systems can be networked, which means that several translators working on the same document or working for the same agency or client can share the same TMs, thereby maintaining consistency within the group. Of course, this type of consistency may not be desirable when working for different clients, since companies may not be content to have their documentation written using a similar style and terminology to that of their competitors. Furthermore, if translation segments for a single target text are leveraged from different clients, text types, or subject fields, the result may be a hodge-podge of styles and terminology.

The change in the way of working brought about by TM technology has also raised questions with regard to quality. As explained in section 5.1, TMs work by matching segments of texts. Therefore, in order for translators to obtain the maximum benefit from TMs, their translations should be similarly segmented. This means that translators who translate sentence-by-sentence, rather than changing the order of sentences or combining or splitting sentences, will improve their chances of finding matches in the TM in future translations. The rigidity of maintaining the same order and number of sentences in the target text as are found in the source text may affect the naturalness and quality of the translation. In addition, a phenomenon referred to as "peephole translation" (Heyn 1998, 135) has been observed, in which translators deliberately formulate texts in such a way as to make them more easily recyclable from a TM. For example, because retrieved matches usually require fewer changes if they do not contain anaphoric and cataphoric references (e.g., pronoun references such as "it" or "this"), translators who are working with TMs may avoid using such structures. This may result in text that is less cohesive and consequently less readable.

Problems such as these have led to concern among some translators that the notion of a "text" has been lost because the tools operate mainly at sentence level. As emphasized in many translation hand-books, such as those by Baker (1992) and Hatim and Mason (1990), sentences cannot be treated in isolation but must be seen as part of the larger text. Consequently, some TM users have switched from sentence-based to paragraph-based segmentation (Esselink 2000, 363). If paragraph-based segments are used, translators can feel free to use anaphoric and cataphoric references or to split or join sentences within a paragraph. Although fewer matches are retrieved for paragraph-based segments than for sentence-based segments, paragraph matches generally require less editing effort than do sentence matches, and the resulting translations are often more readable.

Finally, because a TM is perceived as being less flexible than a word processor (e.g., it requires extra steps to merge two segments or to edit translation units already stored in the TM), some translators may be tempted to do fewer drafts before submitting their final translation, and this may have an impact on the quality of the translation.

5.5.3 Electronic form

As previously mentioned, in order to be stored in a TM, the source text and its translation must first be in electronic form. Although more and more clients are delivering source texts to translators in electronic form, hard copies are still sometimes used. In such cases, a translator must consider whether it is worth converting the hard copy of the text into electronic form in order to use a TM. If the text does not appear to contain internal repetitions, if it is outside of the translator's usual field of specialization, or if it is unlikely to be reused for any other reason, it may not be worth incorporating into the TM. Of course, the difficulty with making such a decision is that translators are unlikely to know at any given moment precisely what source texts they will be faced with in the future. If the translator does decide to convert the text into electronic form, he or she is likely to use OCR or voice recognition. Details of these technologies can be found in sections 2.1 and 2.2.

5.5.4 File formats, filters, and standards

As discussed in section 2.3, different software applications store information in different file formats. TMs are no exception; the format used by any given TM is not necessarily compatible with those of other TMs or of other types of software applications (e.g., various types of word processors, spreadsheets, graphics packages, and databases). To be able to import files from and export files to other formats, TMs must be equipped with filters that allow data to be exchanged between them. Not every TM comes equipped with a filter for every file format in existence, and a translator who wishes to use a TM to assist with the translation of a client's texts must be sure that the TM is able to process the file formats of the source texts in question. Another problem associated with some filters is that information may be lost during the import or export process. Ideally, a filter will extract the translatable text from the original file and present it to the translator in a translation-friendly format, and then once the text has been translated, the filter will convert the file back to its original format with no additional layout work necessary. A good set of filters will attempt to ensure that neither the content nor the formatting information is lost. However, as previously mentioned, filters do not always work perfectly, and translators should test them carefully before exchanging files with clients.

A related problem is that of exchanging data between two different TM systems. Although many packages have some provision for importing and exporting data, the export format of one system does not always match the import format of another. A special-interest group known as OSCAR, which is part of LISA, has developed a standard data-exchange format called Translation Memory eXchange (TMX). TMX designates how segments of text are defined and aligned within TMs, thus allowing these segments to be ported to any other system that supports the standard. The purpose of TMX is to make it easier to import and export data between different TM systems without losing or distorting information.

A standard data-exchange format for TMs would be welcomed by translators. It would mean that they could purchase and use a single TM system, regardless of what systems their clients were using. This would save them both time (e.g., reduced learning curve) and money. Many developers of TM systems are also supportive of this effort, though a few are somewhat less enthusiastic about the prospect. Because it is not currently easy to make the transition from one tool to another, users tend to stay with the tool they have, even though it might not be the cheapest or the most user-friendly, but some developers fear that they might lose customer loyalty once TM data can be read by any TM system.

5.5.5 Character sets and language-related difficulties

Some languages are easier to process than others, so it is important to make sure that the selected TM system is able to process the necessary languages. For example, languages such as Arabic and Hebrew require bidirectional support – these languages are normally displayed and read from right to left, but they also need to be able to display from left to right (e.g., if proper nouns or borrowed words from languages such as English or French are integrated into the text).

Other technical difficulties may arise for translators working with some Asian languages. As explained in section 3.4.6, in most languages, a single character can generally be stored using one byte (i.e., one unit of storage); however, double-byte languages (e.g., Chinese, Japanese, and Korean) require two bytes to store a single character. Unfortunately, many computer applications, including some TM systems, have been written in such a way that they can only process single-byte character sets. This means that translators who work with double-byte character sets may not be able to use certain existing TM systems; we can hope that all future systems will be Unicode compliant and therefore double-byte enabled.

Additional language-related difficulties may arise with regard to segmentation. As outlined in section 5.1.1, in order to create a TM, the system must be able to divide the source text into segments. This means that the system must be able to recognize which elements indicate the end of a segment (e.g., punctuation). When working with languages such as Chinese, Japanese, or Korean, some TM systems have difficulty determining where one segment ends and the next begins. This problem arises primarily when these languages are used for the source text; it is generally easier to use TMs in interactive mode to translate out of languages such as English or French into languages such as Chinese because the segmentation decisions are based on the source language. Most TM developers recognize such problems as significant limitations and are working to resolve them.

5.5.6 Attitudes

In the past, computerized tools were frequently seen as a threat to translators. The awareness of translators and their clients of the potential benefits of using computers to help with translation is growing steadily. Nevertheless, there is still a real need to educate both groups about the actual capabilities of CAT tools. Translators need to be reassured that tools such as TMs can help them with their task by eliminating some of the boring, repetitive work and freeing them up to deal with more interesting challenges (e.g., translations requiring a knowledge of semantics or pragmatics). No translator wants to have the feeling that he or she is going to be replaced by a computer or be reduced to someone who merely has to click on the "OK" button to accept a ready-made translation. Clients need to be made aware of the limitations of the tools. Although they are enthusiastic about the potential for achieving a faster time-to-market, they need to be reminded that the translation is not actually being done by a computer. The translators are still performing a challenging and valuable task, and as such, they need to be treated with respect and paid appropriately for the work they do.

5.5.7 Rates of pay

The idea of reusing translations has led to questions about how much translators should be paid if they use TMs. Some TM systems come equipped with a repetition-analysis module (sometimes called a leverage-analysis module) that compares the new source text against the TM before translation takes place in order to compute the number of matches that are likely to be found, as well as the number of internal repetitions contained in the source text. Some modules can also calculate the number of words and translation units contained in a text, ignoring elements such as HTML tags or software code that could influence the word count. Repetition analysis is playing an increasingly important role in the negotiation of prices for translation work. It is also useful for helping clients or translators to estimate how much time should be scheduled for a particular translation task.

Traditionally, translators have charged by the word, line, or page. However, some clients are now requesting discounts for work completed using a TM, arguing that translators should not be paid the full rate for reusing previous translations. For example, while a client may be willing to pay the full rate for the translation of a segment which has no match in the TM, that client may wish to pay only a proportion of the standard rate to have a translator edit a segment for which a fuzzy match is retrieved (e.g., payment of 40 percent of the standard rate for a 60 percent fuzzy match, payment of 30 percent of the standard rate for a 70 percent fuzzy match). Furthermore, some clients may not want to pay anything at all if an exact match is retrieved, even if this match is the result of an internal repetition.

For their part, translators feel that they should still receive competitive rates for fuzzy and exact matches because these segments still need to be proofread and analyzed in context before they are incorporated into the new translation. In fact, some translators note that the use of a TM can improve consistency, thereby improving the overall quality of the text, and they suggest that perhaps customers should pay extra for this improved quality.

The debate over the rate of pay for fuzzy matches has also led to a debate over the sensitivity thresholds that should be used in TMs (see section 5.1.2.3). Because they pay less for fuzzy matches, clients would prefer to see the sensitivity threshold set at around 50 percent, but translators argue that editing a 50 percent match may take more time than translating the segment from scratch and so they would prefer to see the sensitivity threshold set closer to 80 percent. The two parties often compromise on using sensitivity thresholds of between 60 and 70 percent.

Following on from these debates, one noticeable trend is that many translators are now charging clients by the hour, rather than by the word, line, or page. Another reason for this is that there is often extra work involved in using TMs: pre-processing, file conversion, database maintenance, and so on. A translator who charges by the word may end up doing this type of work for free! Another trend that is beginning to emerge is that clients, who are anxious to take advantage of potentially lower costs and faster turnaround times, are seeking out translators who use TMs. In the near future, translators who are unwilling to incorporate this technology into their work practices may find themselves scrambling for business.

5.5.8 Ownership

Another thorny question that has arisen with the advent of TMs is the question of who owns a TM. Given that a TM can be a valuable resource, both translators and clients are naturally anxious to claim ownership. Translators argue that since they have done the work, they should own it, claiming that the TM would not even exist if they had not gone to the trouble of creating it. In contrast, clients want to protect their intellectual property and do not want their competitors to ultimately benefit from translation work for which they have paid. These clients claim that since they commissioned and paid for the work, they should own it. Both arguments have some merit, and since this is a relatively new concept in the industry, there are no legal precedents governing this issue. Consequently, ownership is sometimes subject to negotiation and should be specifically addressed in contracts so that both parties know where they stand.

It should be pointed out, however, that in cases where clients do take ownership of a TM, they typically make it (and sometimes even a copy of the TM system) available to translators who are hired to work on new projects. In this way, translators can have the benefits of working with a TM even if they did not create it themselves, although some translators find it constraining to have to adopt the style and wording of material that has been previously translated by someone else. Furthermore, this type of arrangement is generally restricted to a particular project and client – a translator could not ethically use the TM and system provided by client A to work on a project for client B.

5.5.9 Integration with other tools

Many of the TM systems available today are integrated with other translation-support tools. For instance, the most popular tools on the market also incorporate powerful terminology-management systems and bilingual concordancers, and some TMs can be integrated with machine-translation systems.

At a more fundamental level, some TMs work with existing word processors, whereas others come with a proprietary text editor. In the former case, a translator opens the source text and creates the target text directly in a third-party word processor (e.g., MS Word or Word-Perfect). This can reduce the translator's learning curve as he or she can continue working within a familiar piece of software. In the latter case, the translator must import files to and export files from the TM's proprietary format using filters. As noted in sections 2.3 and 5.5.4, when converting files, there is a risk that data may be lost or distorted.

5.5.9.1 Terminology-management systems

TM systems often have integrated terminology-management systems. As described in section 5.1.2.4, a TM system compares the source-text segments against the previously translated segments stored in the TM database. At the same time, using a process known as active terminology recognition (see section 4.3), the terminology-management system compares the individual terms contained in each source text segment against the terms contained in the term base. If a term is recognized as being in the term base, the translator's attention is drawn to the fact that an entry exists for this term, and the translator can view the term record and then insert the term from the record directly into the target text. This means that even when no exact or fuzzy matches are found for source-text segments, the translator might at least find some translation equivalents for individual terms in the terminology-management system's term base.

5.5.9.2 Bilingual concordancers

As noted in section 5.1.2.5, there has been some recognition among users and developers of TMs that full-sentence segments may not always be ideal for allowing the maximum amount of reuse of previous translations. Language is indeed repetitive, but much of the repetition tends to take place at the sub-sentence level. Therefore, another feature that has been integrated into some TMs is a bilingual concordancer. As described in section 3.2.2.2, concordancers allow the user to retrieve all instances of a specific search string and view these occurrences in their immediate context. This means that a translator can ask to see all the occurrences of any text fragment (not just a pre-defined segment, which is usually more or less equivalent to a sentence) that appear anywhere in the TM, along with their translation equivalents. This allows the translator to quickly view the search string in context together with its translations, which may not always be the same. As illustrated in figure 5.10, a bilingual concordance search for the pattern "not valid" has retrieved six different occurrences of this string, which has been translated in three different ways, depending on the context.

The two approaches may well be considered complementary, however, and translators may benefit from having access to both types of processing, depending on the nature of the text they are translating (see section 5.4). On the one hand, translators working with texts that contain a large number of repeated segments, such as revisions, will be well served by the segment processing approach. On the other hand, translators who hope to leverage or recycle information from previous translations that are from the same subject field, but that are not revisions, may find that the bilingual concordancing approach is more productive.

5.5.9.3 Machine-translation systems

Finally, some developers are integrating TMs with machine-translation

EN: The specified object is not valid. FR: L'objet spécifié est non valide.
EN: The file identifier is not valid. FR: L'identificateur du fichier n'est pas valide.
EN: The specified file is not valid or does not include the correct data. FR: Le fichier spécifié est non valide ou contient des données incorrectes.
EN: The specified animation is not valid. FR: L'animation spécifiée est non valide.
EN: The default file location is not valid. FR: L'emplacement du fichier par défaut n'est pas valide.
EN: The value entered for the <X> property is not valid. FR: La valeur entrée pour la propriété <X> est incorrecte.

Figure 5.10   A bilingual concordance retrieved from a TM for the search pattern "not valid."

systems. This combination of tools can be used in the following way. A new source text can first be compared against a TM, which will replace those segments for which exact matches are retrieved. The segments that are still untranslated can be fed into a machine-translation system, which produces a draft translation. The entire document is then passed on to a human translator for post-editing. The final translation can then be aligned with the original source text and stored in the TM database for future reuse.

5.5.10 Economic aspects

An important consideration for translators who are thinking about working with TMs is the cost involved. Although TMs have the potential to pay off with increased productivity in the long term, the initial set up costs may be prohibitive, particularly for freelance translators or small translation companies that are operating on limited budgets.

TM systems are relatively sophisticated and have taken considerable time and effort to develop. As a result, good systems can be fairly expensive. Many TM systems sell for several thousand dollars. Moreover, as explained in section 5.5.4, the different TM systems are not necessarily compatible with each other. This means that if a translator has several different clients who use different TM systems, the translator may be faced with the prospect of investing in more than one system. In some cases, a client will defray the cost by purchasing a TM system and providing the translator with access to that system for the duration of the project. Of course, this means that the translator can use the TM system only when working on a specific project or for a specific client, which may mean that the translator might not be able to reap the full long-term benefits that can be gained by building a TM over time.

In addition to the cost of the TM system(s), translators may incur other expenses. For example, although the minimum system requirements for running the software may be low, translators may wish to upgrade their hardware (e.g., processor, memory, storage capacity) to get optimal performance. Moreover, because most TM systems work in split-screen mode (the new source text is displayed on one half of the screen while the contents of the TM are displayed on the other), users are often encouraged to work on 17- or 19-inch monitors (as opposed to the standard 14-inch monitors) so that there will be enough room to display all the information. Finally, if a translation company wishes to allow multiple translators to benefit from using the same TMs, a stable network must be installed and a multi-user licence purchased.

Translators wishing to integrate existing translations into a new TM system may be faced with additional expenses. If the texts are already in electronic format, they will need an alignment program (see section 5.2.2); however, if the texts are in hard copy, they will first need to be converted into electronic format using a scanner and OCR software (see section 2.1) or voice-recognition technology (see section 2.2).

Finally, translators who are not computer gurus and would find it difficult to teach themselves how to set up and effectively use the software, or to trouble-shoot technical problems that may arise, may need to pay additional fees for installation, training and product-support contracts.

All told, these expenditures can be quite significant, and the anticipated return on investment may not materialize as quickly as a translator might hope. Before making a decision to purchase TM software, translators should give careful consideration to factors such as the types of texts they normally translate (section 5.4), how their clients feel about TM systems (see section 5.5.6), and issues of pay (see section 5.5.7) and ownership (see section 5.5.8). The answers to these questions will help them to decide whether the initial set-up costs can be justifiably balanced against the potential long-term gains. Details on some commercially available TMs can be found in Appendix B.

KEY POINTS

- Translation memories (TMs) align source and target texts and store the aligned segments in a database.
- The essential idea behind a TM system is that it allows a translator to reuse previously translated segments. The system automatically compares a new source text against the database of previous translations.
- Segment matching can take place at different levels: exact matching, full matching, fuzzy matching, term matching, or sub-segment matching.
- TMs can be created through interactive translation or through post-translation alignment.
- Not all texts are equally suitable for use with TMs. Texts that are conducive to translation with the help of a TM include updates, revisions, texts with repetitive content, and a series of texts in the same subject field.
- There is evidence to indicate that this technology is bringing about some changes in conventional practice (e.g., translators formulate texts in such a way as to make them more recyclable).
- The use of TMs has raised some controversial issues relating to ownership and rates of pay.
- TMs can often be integrated with other tools, such as word processors, terminology-management systems, bilingual concordancers, and machine-translation systems, thus creating an integrated translator's workbench or workstation.

FURTHER READING

- O'Brien (1998) provides a good introduction to TMs accompanied by a discussion of the benefits and challenges they present to translators and clients.
- Bédard (1998) and L'Homme (1999a, chapter 7) both present a clear summary of the main features of TMs and of important things to know when working with such tools.

- Webb (1998) and L'Homme (1999a, chapter 10) discuss the suitability of different types of texts for use with TMs.
- Heyn (1998) and Trujillo (1999) offer more technical descriptions of how TMs work.
- Esselink (2000, chapter 11) provides descriptions of a number of specific TM tools, including TRADOS, SDLX, STAR TransIT, Déjà Vu and IBM Translation Manager.
- Macklovitch and Russell (2000) address some of the limitations of current TM systems.
- Hofmann and Mehnert (2000) provide a case study in which a TM was used to enable translators to begin translating even before the source text was finalized.
- Melby (1998) discusses the TMX data exchange standard.
- Ahrenberg and Merkel (1996) and Kenny (1999) consider how TMs affect the translation process.
- Rode (2000) discusses issues relating to learning curves, attitudes, and rates of pay for freelance translators who are faced with the use of TMs.
- Topping (2000b) explores issues relating to ownership of TMs and the ethics of sharing TMs.
- Andrés Lange and Bennett (2000) present a case study in which a TM system has been successfully integrated with a machine-translation system.

6. Other New Technologies and Emerging Trends

Language technology is still largely an emerging market.

Fry (2000, 18)

As technology continues to develop, translators must make an effort to keep abreast of changes and advances. At times, this can seem like a full-time job in itself, but it is important if translators wish to remain competitive in the twenty-first-century marketplace. This final chapter will briefly explore a number of other new technologies and emerging trends relating to the impact of technology on the translation profession and vice versa.

6.1 New attitudes toward translation and translators

As the volume of translation increases, translators are depending more and more on technology to help them with their task. In order to maximize the usefulness of technology, it has become necessary to change the way in which the translation process is viewed. In the past, translation was often seen as an "add-on" process, and it was divorced from the principal document-production process. However, it is now becoming increasingly clear that it is more beneficial to integrate these two processes by viewing them as related elements in a larger document-production chain. Technology is now being developed that supports this view of the integrated document-production cycle and makes it easier for authors and translators to work together. For example, an increasing number of clients who are writing documentation with a view to getting the texts translated by translators using technology such as TM systems are beginning to implement more stringent writing and style guidelines. By asking writers to use a sort of controlled language, clients can maximize the recyclability of the texts during the translation process. For instance, as seen in section 5.5.2, techniques such as eliminating anaphora and using preferred terms can increase the number of matches found by a TM. Other suggestions include avoiding ellipses, using punctuation consistently, and preferring the active voice over the passive voice. Tools known as critiquing systems are being developed to check that authors have followed the controlled-language guidelines. Such controlled-language checkers work in a fashion akin to sophisticated spelling and grammar checkers. Of course, controlled language may not be appropriate for all text types, but it can be implemented in some types (e.g., technical manuals), and its potential for improving the value of TMs and machine-translation systems is generating considerable interest.

In addition, as described in section 5.4.4, tools such as TMs make it easier for translators to begin working on documents even before they have been finalized. If an author updates a document, the translator can run the updated source text through the TM system and it will quickly identify new or changed segments. Furthermore, document and work-flow management technology is being used to record the housekeeping history of a document. A document can be "checked out" from a central system in much the same way as a book is checked out from a library. This means that only one person can edit the document at any given time, and when the original is updated, the system can send out notification that the translation also needs to be updated. A related type of management tool is gaining popularity in the software-localization industry, where a single tool can be used to manage all elements of a software-localization project, including translation, quality assurance, and software engineering. This new attitude toward translation and its integration into the document-production process has been facilitated by technology.

As Haynes (1998, 59), Heyn (1998, 135), and Rode (2000, 13) note, an additional change in attitude is starting to be seen among translators themselves. Mastering sophisticated technology can significantly improve the way that translators see themselves, and clients in turn pick up on this positive image. Being able to use new technologies represents an added professional skill for translators, and it is a skill that is becoming increasingly appreciated in the marketplace.

6.2   New types of translation work generated by technology

As the number of electronic products and resources increases, there is a growing demand for translators who are able to translate media such as software applications, multimedia products, Web pages, and even on-line chat sessions. As noted in section 1, software localization, which is the adaptation of a software package to a target language and culture, is one of the fastest-growing translation markets. Although translation is an important component of software localization, it is not the only one; other tasks involved in the localization process include engineering, testing, and project management. With regard to the translation component of software localization, translators must translate or adapt the user interface (e.g., menus, dialogue boxes, icons, buttons), help files, error messages, and accompanying documentation (e.g., user manuals). Although software localization involves many of the same considerations as do other types of translation (e.g., appropriate representation of date, time, and currency formats), it also involves some additional considerations.

One additional issue that translators must deal with is the physical constraints of the screen space. In some development environments, the width of a menu or a button can be adjusted (e.g., to accommodate the longer French term "Sauvegarder" as a translation of the shorter English term "Save"), but in other cases, the width is fixed and the translator must choose a term or a transparent abbreviation that fits within the allocated space.

Similarly, a translator may need to adjust the "hot keys" or "shortcut keys" because these often have mnemonic significance. For example, if an English-language program uses the shortcut "Ctrl-p" to enable users to "print" a document, a translator localizing this product into French might consider changing the shortcut to "Ctrl-i" to create a similar mnemonic reference for the French equivalent "imprimer." Of course, such decisions may have knock-on effects. For instance, it is possible that this shortcut has already been assigned to another function (e.g., "italique"), or technical alterations may need to be made to the underlying code in order to effect such a change.

Icons or other visual elements can also be problematic. For example, whereas an icon showing an open door may transparently capture the notion expressed by the corresponding command "Exit" in English, the transparency would be lost if the translator chose to translate that command into the target language using an equivalent that meant "Quit" or "Terminate."

Variables are another software element that may cause difficulties for translators. A variable is a character or string of characters that acts as a placeholder and is replaced by another, more meaningful string of characters when the relevant software is running. For example, in the sentence "The %s font is not available; the %s font will be substituted," the two "%s" variables will be replaced by relevant text strings when the program is running (e.g., "The <u>Times New Roman</u> font is not available; the <u>Courier</u> font will be substituted"). If a translator chooses to reorder the sentence to read "The %s font will be substituted because the %s font is not available," the program may not insert the variables in the correct place and the intended meaning will be distorted (e.g., "The <u>Times New Roman</u> font will be substituted because the <u>Courier</u> font is not available"). Variable substitution can also result in grammatical errors. For example, in an English sentence such as "The %s has been terminated," the "%s" variable could be replaced at different times by strings such as "program," "service," or "installation" without causing any grammatical problems; however, in French, it is not as straightforward. A translation such as "Le %s a été arrêté" may work for the strings "programme" and "service," but it will not work for "installation," which requires that the article be changed from "Le" to "L'" and that an agreement in gender be made (arrêt<u>ée</u>).

Another localization issue that a translator must keep in mind is standardization. If a particular product belongs to a larger family of products, it may be necessary to standardize the terminology (e.g., to use "Exit" instead of "Quit"). These are just a few of the issues involved in software localization. For more information, readers are referred to works such as Esselink (2000), Fry (2000), and Corbolante and Irmler (2001).

6.3   New technology generated by new types of translation work

The relationship between translation and technology is not one-way. As outlined in the previous section, technology has resulted in new types of translation, such as software localization. In turn, these new types of translation are themselves prompting the creation of additional technologies in order to facilitate translation-related tasks. For instance, many of the tools described in previous sections, such as translation-memory systems, are key tools in the localization process.

```
<HTML>
<BODY>
<P><CENTER><U>EXAMPLE</U></CENTER></P>
<P>This is a <B>simple</B> example of a <FONT SIZE = +4> text
</FONT> that has been <I>encoded</I> using HTML tags.</P>
</BODY>
</HTML>
```

Figure 6.1. A sample of source code for a text that has been encoded in HTML.

EXAMPLE

This is a **simple** example of a text that has been *encoded*
using HTML tags.

Figure 6.2. The text as it would appear on the World Wide Web when viewed using a browser.

In addition, other types of tools are being developed, such as those that check to see if a translation has been truncated (e.g., on a button or menu) because of space restrictions. Other tools have been created to separate out the material that needs to be translated from the software code itself. In the case of Web-page translation, translators receiving the source code must be able to distinguish between the translatable elements and the hypertext markup language (HTML) codes or tags. An illustration of Web-page source code containing both translatable material and tags is given in figure 6.1. The same text as it would appear on the Web when viewed using a browser such as Netscape's Navigator or Microsoft's Internet Explorer is illustrated in figure 6.2.

In this simple example, any text that is part of a tag (i.e., any text between angle brackets) must not be translated. Even though some of the material contained in the tags appears to be in English, it is actually a set of instructions telling the computer how to display this information. If a translator were to translate BODY by CORPS or FONT by POLICE DE CARACTÈRES, the computer would not recognize this language and would return an error message. In this example, the only material that should be translated is the text that will actually be dis-

```
<meta name="description" content="The Best Translation Company
– we can help you meet all your translation-related needs">

<meta name="keywords" content="translation, interpretation, termi-
nology, technical writing, localization, editing, revision">
```

Figure 6.3. Examples of meta tags containing text strings that need to be translated

played on the screen, as shown in figure 6.2. On more sophisticated Web pages, however, there may be some material contained within tags (e.g., descriptions and keywords in meta tags, Alt tags, or button tags, some JavaScript content) that does need to be translated. For instance, as illustrated in figure 6.3, the header of an HTML file contains meta tags that provide special information about a Web page, such as a description of the contents of the page and keywords that enable search engines, such as Alta Vista or Google, to find the page.

In the case of meta tags, some (but not all!) of the text within the angle brackets needs to be translated. In the example presented in figure 6.3, the following text strings contained within the angle brackets must be translated: "The Best Translation Company – we can help you meet all your translation-related needs" and "translation, interpretation, terminology, technical writing, localization, editing, revision."

A translator must be able to identify and translate all relevant material without deleting or distorting the computer code. To this end, different types of software have been developed to assist translators. Some of the simpler software displays the translatable and the non-translatable material in different colours so that translators will know where to focus their attention. More sophisticated software will protect the tags to ensure that they cannot be deleted or edited. A new format, known as OpenTag, has also been developed. As illustrated in table 6.1, it acts as a filter that allows the translatable material to be automatically extracted from the software code and presented to the translator as simple text strings in a separate file. A second file is created to act as a reference file. This is essentially a copy of the original file containing placeholders that indicate where the translated text strings should be reinserted. Once the translator has completed the translations, they are then merged back into their appropriate places in the reference file. This is much easier and faster than manually searching through the code, and there are fewer errors resulting from accidental deletion or distortion of tags. Some TM systems are already beginning to integrate

Table 6.1   Contents of a source file, translatable text extracted from that file, and a reference file containing place-holders

Original source file containing a mixture of translatable text and computer code	``` <HTML> <HEAD> <meta name="description" content="The Best Translation Company – we can help you meet all your translation-related needs"> <meta name="keywords" content="translation, interpretation, terminology, technical writing, localization, editing, revision"> </HEAD> <BODY> <H1>WELCOME! You have arrived at the site of The Best Translation Company!</H1> <P>Please explore our site and let us know how we can help you meet your translation-related needs.</P> </BODY> </HTML> ```
Translatable text that has been automatically extracted from the original file and presented to the translator as simple text strings	T1 The Best Translation Company – we can help you meet all your translation-related needs T2 translation, interpretation, terminology, technical writing, localization, editing, revision T3 WELCOME! You have arrived at the site of The Best Translation Company! T4 Please explore our site and let us know how we can help you meet your translation-related needs.
Reference file containing place-holders that indicate where the translated text should be automatically reinserted	``` <HTML> <HEAD> <meta name="description" content="<ref$T1>"> <meta name="keywords" content="<ref$T2>"> </HEAD> <BODY> <H1><ref$T3></H1> <P><ref$T4></P> </BODY> </HTML> ```

this type of feature. Details on some commercially available localization and Web-page translation tools can be found in Appendix B.

A related type of tool has been developed for counting the number of words to be translated on a Web page. If a translator charges a client by the word, the translator must be able to determine which words will be translated (translatable material) and which will not (most tags). It would be extremely difficult and time consuming to attempt to manually identify and count the number of translatable words in a large Web site. At first glance, it might seem that a simple strategy would be to save a Web page as a text file, which will ignore all the tags, and then use the word-count feature on a word processor. However, a translator who takes this approach may end up losing money because, as we have seen, certain types of tags have translatable material embedded within them. Clients expect this material to be translated, but translators who neglect to count it will not be paid for it. New technology has now been developed that can automatically count the number of translatable words in a Web page or site, including translatable material that is embedded within tags or code, and this will help translators to ensure that they are fully compensated for the work they have done. This type of feature is now being integrated into the repetition-analysis module in some TM systems; however, standalone word-counting tools (for Web pages and other types of files) are also commercially available. Details on some such tools can be found in Appendix B.

6.4 Conditions required to ensure the continued success of CAT tools

As noted throughout this book, CAT tools of all kinds are becoming increasingly popular, and a number of conditions will be critical to ensure the continuation of this trend. Haynes (1998, 136) suggests that more developers of CAT tools should make their products freely available to translator training institutes, noting that these developers may well benefit financially when the students graduate and are in a position to influence corporate purchasing decisions regarding translation technology. He adds that another mutually beneficial opportunity that should be further investigated is that of using translator-training institutes as beta test sites for translation-technology products.

Once translators have access to translation technology, it is essential that both they and their clients be educated with regard to the realistic expectations that they can have for CAT tools. In addition, tools must be made as user-friendly as possible without compromising functionality, and they must be able to run on desktop computers. Some translation memories and terminology-management systems can already be integrated into software environments that are familiar to translators (e.g., word processors). Other tools, such as word-counting and Web-page translation tools, shield translators from the messy business of wading through computer code and allow them to focus on identifying and translating the relevant text strings. The advantage of this approach is that it helps to reduce the translator's learning curve, which makes the translator more receptive to using the tools.

Since the texts to be processed using CAT tools must be in electronic form, it will be of great help to translators if clients supply these texts in electronic form rather than hard copy. This would eliminate the need for translators to convert hard-copy texts using technology such as OCR or voice recognition (see sections 2.1 and 2.2). Some clients are already providing translators with electronic source texts, but those who are not yet doing this should be encouraged to start.

As mentioned in section 6.1, some clients are implementing a sort of controlled language in their document production process, and they are integrating translation into the document production cycle. These changes will help to maximize the usefulness of some types of CAT tools.

Finally, it is important to continue working toward the development and implementation of standards that will enable users to exchange data and to move between different systems more easily.

6.5   Future developments

What future developments are we likely to see with regard to CAT tools? With regard to TMs in particular, there has been concern among translators that the notion of a "text" has been lost because the tools operate primarily at sentence level. As discussed in section 5.5.2, this has raised concerns about the quality of translations produced using TMs (e.g., the lack of cohesion and reduced readability of "peephole translations"). Macklovitch and Russell (2000, 145) also point out that a text has global properties that are not easily associated with its lower-level components, including administrative information concerning who originally translated a text, the date of the translation, the client, and so on. This type of information applies to the text as a whole, rather than to each individual segment, but most current TM systems provide little or no support for document management and archiving. If a TM had the ability to represent documents explicitly, or could at least reconstruct documents from the segments, users would be able to do things such as search on administrative information (e.g., to find the most recent text translated for a particular client), retrieve similar texts and their translations for background reading before starting a new project, process extended passages (instead of just sentence-based segments), or examine larger contexts in which proposed matches for the current segment appear. It is likely that new versions of TM tools will take these needs into account, either by building document-management features directly into TMs, or by allowing TMs to be integrated with existing document-management systems.

In terms of more general developments, it is likely that there will be a continued movement away from stand-alone systems (i.e., systems that run on a single computer) and toward a client-server architecture, which facilitates networking, thus making it possible for multiple users to share the same corpora, TMs, or term bases. Along similar lines, there is also an interest in developing online translation editors that would allow multiple translators to share TMs over the Internet. This will be particularly appealing to freelance translators.

Other improvements that are underway include extending CAT tools to support a wider variety of languages (e.g., Thai, Urdu) by using encoding methods such as Unicode, and designing new standards and filters to support a wider variety of file formats, including formats using tags (e.g., HTML, XML), without losing the formatting of the original source text.

It is also expected that there will be increasing integration of a variety of CAT tools to create a collection of integrated computer aids for translators that is sometimes referred to as a translator's workbench or workstation. This will be accompanied by an increased use of the generated resources (e.g., corpora, TMs, term bases) as a foundation for developing machine translation systems (e.g., EBMT systems) and other natural-language processing tools.

As the number of different tools increases, one further challenge facing translators is learning how to evaluate and exploit the strengths of each of these tools. Cost/benefit estimators have been developed that can help translators to try to calculate whether or not it will be worth their while to use a certain type of tool, or even a particular product. Even more sophisticated is a new type of tool, sometimes referred to as a diagnostic tool or a translation router, that is being developed to help translators or translation project managers to decide whether a given document should be translated by an unaided human translator, a human translator using CAT tools, or a machine-translation system. Ahrenberg and Merkel (1996, 192) describe how diagnostic tools can be used to determine text profiles, which in turn can be used to help translators decide which (if any) tool to use for translating a particular text. For instance, it has already been noted in section 5.4.1 that texts containing a high number of internal repetitions are particularly conducive to being translated with the help of a TM. One such diagnostic tool, known as TransRouter, is currently under development by a European Union–funded consortium (Cleary and Schäler 2000). TransRouter will evaluate the usefulness of available resources in the context of a specific translation project based on information supplied by the user (e.g., a translator or translation manager) and on the automatic analysis of text characteristics using its component features. These component features will include a cost estimator, a word counter, a version comparer, a repetition analyzer, an unknown-term detector, a sentence-length estimator, and a sentence-simplicity checker. Following this evaluation, TransRouter will suggest possible translation routes for a particular project providing details on time, cost, and quality implications. The development of such a tool promises to be of benefit to translators and managers of translation projects, especially those who have to deal with large numbers of documents to be translated. This type of tool aims to ease the pressure of decision making and reinforce confidence in the appropriateness of that decision.

KEY POINTS

- Translation is becoming increasingly integrated into the broader document-production process.
- As technology advances, new types of translation work are being created (e.g., software localization, Web page translation).
- These new types of translation work, in turn, are prompting the development of new types of technology (e.g., software for separating translatable text from tags, software for counting translatable elements in a text).
- A number of conditions can be implemented to ensure the continued success of CAT tools: users must be educated with regard to reasonable expectations, tools must be user friendly, source texts should be supplied in electronic form, controlled languages can be employed, developers can work more closely with translator-training institutes.
- Future developments in CAT technology include a movement toward client-server architectures, extensions to support more languages and file formats, further integration of tools, further use of generated resources to develop other natural-language processing tools, and the development of diagnostic tools.

FURTHER READING

- Hofmann and Mehnert (2000) present a case study in which translation has been successfully integrated into the document production process.
- Lockwood (2000) discusses controlled language and the integration of authoring and translation tools.
- Fry (2000) provides a general introduction to the software-localization industry.
- Esselink (2000) and Corbolante and Irmler (2001) outline practical tips for translators and terminologists working in the software-localization industry.
- Kohlmeier (2000) and Sprung and Vourvoulias-Bush (2000) provide case studies of localization projects in which document and workflow management tools proved to be invaluable.
- Cheng (2000) provides a case study that outlines some of the challenges associated with translating a Web site.
- Heyn (1998) makes some general predictions about future developments for CAT tools, while Macklovitch and Russell (2000) make some predictions about the future development of translation memories.
- Ahrenberg and Merkel (1996) and Cleary and Schäler (2000) present information about diagnostic tools.

Glossary

active terminology recognition: A type of automatic dictionary lookup. The terminology-recognition component compares items in the source text against the contents of the term base, and if a match is found, the term record in question is displayed for the translator to consult. See also: **pre-translation.**

algorithm: A series of steps that are undertaken to solve a problem.

alignment: The process whereby sections of a source text are linked up with their corresponding translations. Alignment can take place at many different levels: text, paragraph, sentence, sub-sentence chunk, or even word. Automatic alignment tools are available to help with this process.

alignment "on the fly": The process whereby alignment is carried out during the generation of bilingual concordances rather than being carried out as a separate process (i.e., before the generation of bilingual concordances).

anaphoric reference: When a word refers back to a preceding word or group of words (e.g., a pronoun that can be linked to a preceding noun). See also: **cataphoric reference.**

annotation: The process of encoding additional linguistic information into a corpus. This information can be syntactic (e.g., part-of-speech tags) or semantic (e.g., distinguishing between different meanings of a word). Syntactic annotation can be done automatically using a special piece of software known as a tagger. See also: **mark-up**.

ASCII (American Standard Code for Information Interchange): A standard 7-bit character set developed by the American National Standards Institute (ANSI) that is used to represent 128 characters which include the Roman alphabet, Arabic numerals, and a selection of other symbols that appear on most keyboards (e.g., ! ? $ % &). ASCII is a commonly recognized character set in a variety of applications because it is very basic (e.g., it does not allow formatting such as bold or italics). Although the original ASCII uses 7 bits, the common storage unit consists of 8 bits (totalling one byte), which allows 256 characters to be represented. In 8-bit ASCII (also known as extended ASCII), the first 7 bits follow the ANSI standard, but the extra bit is used differently depending on the computer (e.g., in the PC the additional values are used for foreign language and graphics symbols, but in the Macintosh the additional values can be user-defined).

batch translation mode: A method of interacting with a translation memory (TM) in which a user runs the complete source text through the system and whenever it finds an exact match, it automatically replaces the new source text segment with the translation that is stored in the TM. Segments for which no match is found in the TM must later be translated by either a human translator or a machine translation system. See also: **interactive translation mode, pre-translation**.

bidirectional language: A language such as Arabic or Hebrew that is displayed and read from right to left, but that can also support left-to-right display (e.g., for words or names borrowed from left-to-right languages such as English).

bilingual comparable corpus: A two-part corpus in which both parts contain texts that have the same communicative function, but one part contains texts originally written in language A while the other contains texts originally written in language B. Because the two collections do not have a source text-target text relationship, they cannot be aligned. See also: **monolingual comparable corpus**.

bilingual concordancer: A type of corpus analysis tool that operates on an aligned parallel corpus by retrieving all the occurrences of a particular search pattern and its immediate context (usually a segment such as a sentence or paragraph) along with its corresponding translation segments. See also: **monolingual concordancer.**

bitext: See **parallel corpus.**

Boolean operator: A query limiter such as AND, OR, or NOT that can be incorporated into a search pattern to restrict the list of returned results (e.g., search for all occurrences of "laser" AND "printer").

byte: A common unit of computer storage made up of 8 binary digits (bits). The individual characters of most languages can be stored in a single byte. See also: **double-byte character set.**

CAT: See **computer-aided translation.**

cataphoric reference: When a word refers to another word or group of words that follow (e.g., a demonstrative pronoun such as "this" which can be linked to a noun that comes later in the text). See also: **anaphoric reference.**

character set: A group of unique symbols used for display and printing. Different character sets may be needed for different alphabets or languages. See also: **double-byte character set.**

collocation: Words that co-occur with a greater than random probability (i.e., words that are often "found in each other's company").

command/control voice-recognition system: A voice-recognition system that allows users to interact with the computer by giving a limited set of commands, which usually correspond to the commands found on application menus (e.g., "Open," "Copy," "Paste"). See also: **dictation voice recognition system.**

comparable corpus: See **monolingual comparable corpus** and **bilingual comparable corpus.**

compression: The process used to reduce the size of a computer file by eliminating data redundancies.

computer-aided translation (CAT): The process whereby human translators use computerized tools to help them with translation-related tasks. See also: **machine translation.**

concordancer: See **monolingual concordancer** and **bilingual concordancer.**

context-sensitive search: A concordance search in which another term must appear within a user-specified distance of the search pattern (e.g., contexts in which "access" appears within five words of "Internet").

continuous voice-recognition system: A voice-recognition system that allows users to dictate text at a normal speaking rate without pausing between each word. See also: **discrete voice-recognition system.**

controlled language: A simplified subset of natural language that has a restricted vocabulary and syntax. Controlled language promotes consistency and reduces ambiguity; therefore, texts written in a controlled language can be more easily processed by a machine-translation system or will achieve a greater number of matches when a translation-memory system is used.

conversion: See **file conversion.**

corpus: A large collection of electronic texts that have been gathered according to specific criteria. See also: **bilingual comparable corpus, monolingual comparable corpus, parallel corpus.**

corpus-analysis tools: Software that allows users to access and display the information contained within a corpus in a variety of useful ways. Most corpus-analysis tools typically contain a number of useful features that allow users to generate and manipulate word-frequency lists, concordances, and collocations.

critiquing system: A computer program that advises users with regard to the appropriateness of decisions that they have made. For example, a critiquing system could be used to check whether or not users have followed guidelines correctly when writing in a controlled language.

DBCS: See **double-byte character set.**

derivation: The process of adding a prefix or suffix to an existing word in order to produce a new word which often has a different part of speech (e.g., adding the suffix "ish" to the noun "boy" produces the adjective "boyish"). See also: **inflection**.

diagnostic tool: A tool that analyzes a given source text and helps translators decide what (if any) tools should be used when translating that text.

dictation voice-recognition system: A voice-recognition system that allows users to enter new data into the computer by dictation instead of typing. See also: **command/control voice-recognition system, continuous voice-recognition system, discrete voice-recognition system**.

discrete voice-recognition system: A dictation voice-recognition system in which the user must pause between words so that the computer can distinguish where one word ends and the next begins. For most speakers, this entails modifying their normal way of speaking, reducing it to a slower and more stilted pace. See also: **continuous voice-recognition system**.

double-byte character set (DBCS): A character set that requires two bytes to store a single character (e.g., for languages such as Chinese, Japanese, Korean).

elision: The omission of sounds, syllables, or words in connected speech, as in such forms as *fish'n'chips* or *Febr'y.* Languages that contain a great deal of elision may be harder for voice-recognition systems to process.

encoding: The process of converting the contents of a file into ASCII text so that the characters will be preserved when the file is transmitted (e.g., as an e-mail attachment).

exact match: A segment retrieved by a translation memory that is 100 percent identical (both linguistically and in terms of formatting) to a segment in the new source text that the translator is currently translating. See also: **full match, fuzzy match, sub-segment match, term match**.

example-based machine translation (EBMT): An approach to machine translation in which chunks of the new source text are automatically compared against a corpus of previously translated material in order to find suitable equivalents.

export: To save a copy of the current file into the file format required by a different application. Note that the conversion process may not be perfect. See also: **import**.

eXtensible Markup Language (XML): A markup language containing tags or symbols that are used to describe data elements on a Web page. XML uses a similar tag structure to HTML; however, whereas HTML defines how data elements are displayed, XML defines what those elements contain. HTML uses predefined tags, but XML allows tags to be defined by the developer of the page. Thus, virtually any data items, such as source text, client, and translator, can be identified, allowing Web pages to function like database records. XML was developed by the World Wide Web Consortium (http://www.w3.org).

external repetitions: Segments of text stored in a translation memory that correspond to segments found in previously translated texts. See also: **internal repetitions, recycling**.

file conversion: Changing a file from one format to another. See also: **export, import**.

file format: The layout and organization of information in a file. There are hundreds of proprietary formats, and specific applications typically need a file to be organized in a certain way in order to be able to read the information in it. See also: **proprietary format**.

filter: A conversion routine that changes one data format into another.

format: See **file format**.

formatted text: Text that contains codes for font changes, headers, footers, margins, indents, bold, italics, and other character and document attributes.

frequency threshold: The minimum number of times that an item (or series of items) must occur before it is acted upon by a system.

full match: A segment retrieved from a translation memory (TM) that differs from a stored TM unit only in terms of variable elements (e.g., numbers, dates, times, currencies). See also: **exact match, fuzzy match, sub-segment match, term match, variable element.**

fuzzy match: A segment retrieved from a translation memory that is similar, but not identical, to the segment of the new source text that is being translated. See also: **exact match, full match, sub-segment match, term match.**

hit list: A list of all term records that match a specified search pattern (e.g., when using a wildcard or fuzzy search). From this list, users can select the record(s) they wish to view.

homograph: A word that has the same spelling as another word but has a different part of speech. For example, the word "cook" can be either a noun or a verb.

homonym: A word that has the same spelling and part of speech as another word but has a different meaning. For example, the word "bank" can be used to refer to a financial institution or to the side of a river.

homophone: A word that has the same pronunciation as another word but is spelled differently and has a different meaning. For example, the words "mail" and "male" are homophones.

hot key: a keystroke or combination of keystrokes that can be used to activate a command or option (e.g., "Ctl-s" is the hot key for "Save" in Microsoft products).

HTML: See **hypertext markup language.**

hypertext markup language (HTML): The markup language used to define the document display format for the World Wide Web. Web pages are built with HTML tags, or markup symbols, embedded in the text. HTML defines the page layout, fonts, and graphic elements as well as the hypertext links to other documents on the Web.

import: To read a file in a format that was created by a different application to the one in use. See also: **export.**

inflection: The process used to make a noun plural (e.g., "girl" + "s" = "girls") or to conjugate a verb (e.g., "laugh" + "ed" = "laughed"). There is no change in part of speech. See also: **derivation**.

interactive translation mode: A method of interacting with a translation memory (TM) in which translators add translation units to the TM as they go along. Each time the translator translates a source-text segment, the paired translation unit (the source text segment and its equivalent translation) is stored in the TM database. Once a segment has been translated and stored, it immediately becomes part of the TM and can be reused for future translations. See also: **batch translation mode**.

internal repetitions: Repeated segments occurring within a single source text. See also: **external repetitions, propagation**.

key word in context (KWIC): A method of displaying concordance lines in which all occurrences of the search word are centred on the screen surrounded by the immediate context.

KWIC: See **key word in context**.

lemma: A word in a corpus that is used to include and represent all related forms (e.g., all the conjugations of a verb).

leveraging: See **recycling**.

liaison: The introduction of a sound at the end of a word in certain phonological contexts. For example, a final consonant may be introduced before a following vowel, as in the French phrase "vous allez," where the "s" in "vous" is pronounced (as compared to "vous venez," where the "s" is not pronounced). Languages that contain a great deal of liaison may be more difficult for voice-recognition systems to process.

localization: The process of customizing or adapting a product for a target language and culture. The term localization is sometimes abbreviated to L10N, where 10 indicates the number of letters that come between the 'L' and the 'N'. See also: **Localization Industry Standards Association, software localization**.

Localization Industry Standards Association (LISA): A private, non-profit organization that aims to promote the localization industry and provide a mechanism and services to enable companies to exchange and share information on the development of processes, tools, technologies, and business models connected with localization (http://www.lisa.org). See also: **localization, Open Standards for Container/Content Allowing Reuse.**

machine translation (MT): The process whereby a computer has the primary responsibility for the translation of a text. A human may assist in the process through such tasks as pre- or post-editing, but it is the computer, rather than the human, that produces an actual draft translation. See also: **computer-aided translation.**

mark up: To encode additional non-linguistic information into an electronic text (e.g., information about the structural divisions of a text). See also: **annotation.**

MI: See **mutual information.**

monolingual comparable corpus: A two-part corpus in which one part contains a collection of texts that have been originally written in language A, and the second part contains a collection of similar texts that have been translated into language A from other languages. See also: **bilingual comparable corpus.**

monolingual concordancer: A tool that operates on a monolingual corpus by retrieving all the occurrences of a particular search pattern in its immediate contexts and displaying these in an easy-to-read format such as a KWIC display. See also: **bilingual concordancer.**

MT: See **machine translation.**

multi-word unit: A group of two or more words used to express a single concept (e.g., "disk drive", "part of speech").

mutual information (MI): A formula used to determine the strength of the relationship between two words. The MI score between any given pair of words compares the probability that two words appear together as a unit against the probability that their co-occurrence is simply a result of chance. If two words have a high MI score, they are strongly connected (i.e., they are likely to be collocates); if they have a low MI score, they are not strongly connected.

named entity: See **variable element.**

node: The lexical item whose behaviour is under investigation (e.g., the search pattern).

noise: Items that are retrieved during a search but that are not of interest. See also: **silence.**

OCR: See **optical character recognition.**

"on the fly": See **alignment "on the fly."**

Open Standards for Container/Content Allowing Reuse (OSCAR): A LISA special-interest group responsible for developing standard data exchange formats for translation memory systems and term bases. See also: **Term Base eXchange, Translation Memory eXchange.**

OpenTag: A format that supports the extraction of translatable text from computer code and the reinsertion of the translated text back into its proper place in the code (http://www.opentag.com).

optical character recognition (OCR): The conversion of characters into an electronic form that can be manipulated in other applications such as word processors.

OSCAR: See **Open Standards for Container/Content Allowing Reuse.**

parallel corpus: A corpus containing source texts aligned with their translations.

parsing: The process of analyzing a sentence to determine its formal or functional constituents (e.g., adjective, noun, verb or subject, predicate, object).

"peephole translation": A translation that has been formulated in such a way as to make it more easily recyclable from a translation memory (e.g., pronoun references may have been eliminated) with the result that the text as a whole may be less cohesive and consequently less readable.

phoneme: A distinct, non-divisible unit of sound.

placeable: See **variable element**.

plain text: See **ASCII**.

pre-translation: A feature offered by some terminology-management/ translation-memory (TM) systems in which terms/segments in the source text for which an exact match is found in the term base/TM will be automatically replaced, resulting in a partially translated or hybrid text that must be post-edited by a translator. See also: **batch translation mode**.

propagation: Reusing an internal repetition when working with a translation memory. See also: **internal repetitions, recycling**.

proprietary format: A file format that has been created using a specific software application and can therefore only be read by a copy of the same application that was used to create the file in the first place. See also: **file format**.

recycling: Reusing sections of previous translations when translating a new source text with the help of a translation memory. See also: **external repetitions, propagation**.

regular expression: A group of characters, some of which have special meaning, that can be processed by a computer. For example, the regular expression "^s[a|e|i|o|u]ng" could be used to search for all words that begin with the letter "s" followed by any vowel and end with the letters "ng." This search would likely retrieve occurrences of words such as "sing," "sang," "song," and "sung." Other examples of regular expressions include wildcard searches (e.g., "scan*" to find "scanner," "scanning," etc.) and case-sensitive searches (e.g., "= =Polish= =" to find "Polish" but not "polish").

repetition analysis: The process of analyzing a new source text and comparing it against the translation memory before translation takes place in order to compute the number of matches that are likely to be found, as well as the number of internal repetitions contained in the source text.

revision: An amended version of a previous text. Translation memories are particularly useful in translating this type of text. See also: **update**.

Rich Text Format (RTF): A file format that allows the user to transfer formatted text and graphics from one word processor to another. It attempts to retain the formatting features of the original text, but sometimes the more complex formatting is distorted or lost.

RTF: see **Rich Text Format**.

scanner: A device that reads a printed page and converts it into a graphics image for the computer. The scanner does not recognize the content of the printed material it is scanning. Everything on the page (text and graphics objects) is converted into a single graphics image.

segment: A predefined unit of a text that can be aligned with its corresponding translation. Typically, the basic unit of segmentation is a sentence, but other units can also be defined as segments, such as headings, items in a list, cells in a table, or paragraphs.

sensitivity threshold: The percentage of a match that must be achieved in order for a segment stored in the translation memory to qualify as a fuzzy match for a segment in the new source text.

shortcut key: See **hot key**.

silence: Items that are of interest but that are not retrieved during a search because the query was not well formulated or comprehensive enough. See also: **noise**.

simship: An abbreviation of "simultaneous shipment," which refers to the practice of releasing multiple language versions of a product at the same time (or at least as close to the same time as is possible).

simultaneous shipment: See **simship.**

software localization: The process of adapting a software product to a target language and culture. From a translator's point of view, this could include the adaptation of a user interface (e.g., menus, dialogue boxes, icons, buttons), help files, error messages, and accompanying documentation (e.g., user manuals). See also: **localization, Localization Industry Standards Association.**

speaker-dependent voice-recognition system: A voice-recognition system that individual users must train by enunciating a collection of text samples to allow the computer to build up a profile of each user's speech patterns. See also: **speaker-independent voice-recognition system.**

speaker-independent voice-recognition system: A voice-recognition system that does not need to be trained by individual users. See also: **speaker-dependent voice-recognition system.**

speech recognition: See **voice recognition.**

speech synthesis: A computer's ability to produce sound that resembles human speech. See also: **voice recognition.**

stop list: A list of items to be ignored by the computer when processing a corpus.

sub-segment match: A match between two chunks of text in a translation memory; these chunks do not constitute a segment or a term (e.g., "cannot be completed because"). See also: **exact match, full match, fuzzy match, term match.**

tag: A sort of label attached to a data element that contains information related to that element (e.g., information about what it is or how it should be displayed). For instance, a tag could contain a formatting code indicating that a particular word should be displayed in italics, or information relating to a particular word in a text (e.g., its part of speech). A set of tags is sometimes referred to as markup, and in the HTML and XML markup languages, tags are enclosed in angle brackets (e.g., <ITALICS>).

tagging: See **annotation.**

TBX: See **Term Base eXchange.**

term base: A collection of term records that can be searched electronically.

Term Base eXchange (TBX): A standard data-exchange format for term bases that is under development by OSCAR.

term-extraction tool: A tool that attempts to analyze texts and automatically extract candidate terms. These candidates must later be verified by a human.

term-identification tool: See **term-extraction tool.**

term match: A match between an individual term in a new source text segment and a term for which there is an entry in the term base. See also: **active terminology recognition, exact match, full match, fuzzy match, sub-segment match.**

term-recognition tool: See **term-extraction tool.**

terminology-management system (TMS): A software application that allows users to create, store, and retrieve term records.

TM: See **translation memory.**

TMS: See **terminology management system.**

TMX: See **Translation Memory eXchange.**

token: An individual word in a corpus. The total number of tokens is equal to the total number of words in a corpus. See also: **type.**

trained voice-recognition system: See **speaker-dependent voice-recognition system.**

translation memory (TM): A type of linguistic database that is used to store and retrieve source texts and their translations so that translators can reuse segments of previous translations when translating a new source text.

Translation Memory eXchange (TMX): A standard data-exchange format for translation memories that was developed by OSCAR.

translation router: See **diagnostic tool**.

translation unit: A source text segment and its corresponding translation as stored in a translation memory.

translator's workbench: A collection of integrated computer aids for translators.

translator's workstation: See **translator's workbench**.

type: A word form in a corpus, each instance of which is referred to as a token. A word frequency list shows how many times each type occurs in a corpus (i.e., how many tokens there are of a given type).

Unicode: A superset of the ASCII character set that uses two bytes to encode each character rather than one. Able to handle 65,536 character combinations rather than just 128 or 256, it can house the alphabets and symbols of most of the world's languages. Unicode was developed by the Unicode Consortium (http://www.unicode.org).

universal voice-recognition system: See **speaker-independent voice-recognition system**.

update: A change in the source text that is made while the translation is still in progress. See also: **revision**.

variable: A character or string of characters that acts as a placeholder and is replaced by another more meaningful character or string of characters when the computer program is running.

variable element: An element such as a number, date, time, currency, measurement, or proper name that typically requires some kind of special treatment in a text but does not generally affect the way in which the rest of the text is translated. See also: **full match**.

voice recognition: The processing of spoken words by a computer. This technology allows a user to interact with a computer by speaking to the computer instead of using a keyboard or mouse. See also: **command/control voice-recognition system, continuous voice-recognition system, dictation voice-recognition system, discrete voice-recognition system, speaker-dependent voice-recognition system, speaker-independent voice-recognition system.**

wildcard: A character that can be used to represent one or more characters in a search string. For example, in many programs, an asterisk can be used to represent a string of characters such that a search using the pattern "translat*" would retrieve "translate," "translated," "translates," "translating," "translation," "translationese," "translations," "translator," "translators," and so on.

word-frequency list: A list of the number of types and tokens contained in a corpus.

XML: see **eXtensible Markup Language.**

zipping: see **compression.**

Some Commercially Available CAT Tools

The purpose of this appendix is to provide a starting point for users who are potentially interested in purchasing commercially available CAT tools. The appendix is divided into sections according to different types of tools: OCR software, voice-recognition software, conversion software, corpus-analysis software, terminology-management and translation-memory systems, localization and Web-page translation tools, word-counting tools, and cost/benefit estimators. Each section begins with a list of questions that potential buyers might consider asking vendors in order to establish whether a particular product meets their needs, and this is followed by a brief description of various commercially available tools. The selection presented here is intended to be representative rather than exhaustive. The details pertaining to the listed products are current as of November 2001, and the prices given are exclusive of taxes or shipping costs. For some of the products, there are also links to online reviews. These links have been included solely for the interest of readers; they express the personal opinions of the reviewers and should not be seen as an endorsement by the present author of any particular product. In some cases, the reviews may not be for the most recent version of a given product, but they may nevertheless be helpful for readers who are looking for a starting point for evaluating different products.

B.1 OCR software

Some questions to ask vendors when choosing OCR software to meet your needs:

- What is the accuracy rate when working with high-quality originals?
- What is the average amount of time required to process one page?
- What languages and character sets are supported?
- What file formats are supported?
- What formatting features are supported (e.g., fonts, tables, lists, columns)?
- Does the software work in conjunction with a dictionary?
- What are the system requirements (e.g., operating system, hardware)?
- What is the cost of the software/upgrades/technical support?
- Who are some of your current clients/users? Can I contact them to ask their opinion about your product?

Product name:	ABBYY FineReader 5.0
Web site:	http://www.abbyy.com/products/fine/index.htm
Price:	US $99 (pro edition), US $399 (office edition)
System requirements:	• Windows 95/98/NT/2000/ME • Intel 486 or higher (Pentium 133 or higher recommended) • 32 MB RAM • 40 MB free hard disk space for minimal program installation • 50 MB free hard disk space for program operation • CD-ROM drive
Online reviews:	• http://www.vnunet.com/Products/1116542 • http://www.abbyy.com/company/test.htm

Product name:	OmniPage Pro 10
Web site:	http://www.scansoft.com/products/omnipage/pro/
Price:	US $499

System requirements:	• Windows 95/98/NT 4.0/2000 • Pentium or higher • 32 MB RAM minimum • 50 MB free hard disk space (90 MB recommended) • CD-ROM drive
Additional comments:	• Recognizes 13 Western European languages • Claims 99%+ accuracy
Online reviews:	• http://www.pcworld.com.hk/comparison/comp0799.htm • http://www.zdnet.com/anchordesk/talkback_qr/story_main_1621.html • http://www.scansoft.com/products/omnipage/pro/users.asp

Product name:	TextBridge Pro Millennium
Web site:	http://www.scansoft.com/products/tbpmill/
Price:	US $79
System requirements:	• Windows 95/98/NT 4.0/2000/ME • 486 or higher • 24 MB RAM minimum (32 MB recommended) • 40 MB free hard disk space
Additional comments:	• Supports 56 languages • Macintosh version available
Online reviews:	• http://www.scansoft.com/products/tbpmill/tbpmillexperts.asp

B.2 Voice-recognition software

Some questions to ask vendors when choosing voice-recognition software to meet your needs:

• Is this product a command/control system or a dictation system?
• Is this product speaker dependent or speaker independent?
• If it is speaker dependent, what type of training is required?

- What is the accuracy rate with/without training?
- Can the system be trained by multiple users?
- If it is a dictation system, does it work with discrete or continuous speech?
- What languages are supported?
- What file formats are supported (e.g., for export)?
- Does the system have an audio playback feature?
- What are the system requirements (e.g., operating system, hardware)?
- Is any hardware included with the product (e.g., microphone, headset)?
- What dictionaries are included with the system? What other ready-made dictionaries are available? How many new words can be added to the dictionaries?
- Does the system use a proprietary text editor or can it be integrated with existing editors (e.g., MS Word, WordPerfect)?
- What is the cost of the product/upgrades/technical support?
- Who are some of your current clients/users? Can I contact them to ask their opinion about your product?

Product name:	IBM Via Voice (Pro Edition)
Web site:	http://www-4.ibm.com/software/speech/ millennium/ professional.html
Price:	US $190
System requirements:	• Operating system: versions available for Windows family, Mac, and Linux • Pentium 233MHz and 256K L2 cache (or higher) • 48 MB RAM • 310 MB free hard disk space • sound board supporting16-bit recording (with microphone jack) • CD-ROM drive
Additional comments:	• Speaker dependent • Continuous dictation • Versions also available for French, German, and Spanish • Via Voice Legal Vocabulary (US $149) • Via Voice Medical Vocabulary (US $149)

Online reviews:	• http://www-4.ibm.com/software/speech/news/20001017-cn.html • http://www.zdnet.com/pcmag/firstlooks/9806/f980630b.html • http://www.ldonline.org/ld_indepth/technology/speech_recog.html

Product name:	L&H Dragon Naturally Speaking
Web site:	http://www.lhsl.com/naturallyspeaking/
Price:	US $199 (preferred edition), US $695 (professional edition)
System requirements:	• Windows 98/NT 4.0/2000/ME • Pentium (266 MHz minimum) • 64 MB RAM minimum (128 MB for professional edition) • 150 MB free hard disk space (195 MB for professional edition); additional 20-50 MB is required for each additional user • sound card • CD-ROM drive
Additional comments:	• Speaker dependent • Continuous dictation • Playback feature • L&H DNS Legal Solutions (US $995) • L&H DNS Medical Solutions (US $995) • L&H DNS Public Safety Solutions (US $795)
Online reviews:	• http://www.compukiss.com/reviews/softrev/dragon/dragon.html • http://www.pcwindia.com/2001jan/techreview6.htm

Product name:	L&H Voice Xpress Professional
Web site:	http://www.lhsl.com/voicexpress/
Price:	US $149.99

System requirements:	• Windows 95/98/2000/NT 4.0 • Pentium II 266MHz with MMX • 64 MB RAM (Windows 98), 96 MB RAM (Windows 2000/NT) • 250 MB free hard disk space • sound board supporting 16-bit 22KHz recording • CD-ROM drive • Noise-cancelling headset microphone (included)
Additional comments:	• Speaker dependent • Continuous dictation • Versions also available for French, German, and Spanish
Online reviews:	• http://www.zdnet.co.uk/pcdir/content/2000/12/software/gr-voice-rec/l-and-h.html • http://www.cnet.com/software/0-3227838-1204-1590468.html • http://shopping.yahoo.com/shop?d=zswv&id=1990385889&cf=4

B.3 Conversion software

Some questions to ask vendors when choosing conversion software to meet your needs:
• What file formats are supported?
• What are the system requirements (e.g., operating system, hardware)?
• What formatting features are supported (e.g., tables, lists, columns, fonts)?
• What is the cost of the product/upgrades/technical support?
• Who are some of your current clients/users? Can I contact them to ask their opinion about your product?

Product name:	Conversions Plus
Web site:	http://www.dataviz.com/products/conversionsplus/index.html

Price:	US $69.95 (single-user licence)
System requirements:	• Windows 95/98/NT 4.0/2000/ME • 20 MB free hard disk space
Additional comments:	• Includes conversion from Macintosh to PC • Converts between a wide range of word-processing, spreadsheet, database, graphics, compression, and encoding formats • Most document formatting is retained
Online reviews:	• http://www.smallmarketradio.com/ sw_conversionsplus.htm • http://www.winmag.com/reviews/software/ 2000/10/1017.htm • http://www.computertimes.com/ oct00edchoiceconversionsplus.htm

Product name:	MacLink Plus Deluxe
Web site:	http://www.dataviz.com/products/ maclinkplus/index.html
Price:	US $99.95 (single-user licence)
System requirements:	• Power PC Macintosh • System 8.1 and above • 8 MB RAM (minimum) • 25 MB free hard disk space
Additional comments:	• Converts between a wide variety of word-processing, spreadsheet, database, graphics, compression, and encoding formats
Online reviews:	• http://www.applelinks.com/reviews/ maclinkplus.shtml • http://maccentral.macworld.com/news/0010/ 26.maclink.shtml

Product name:	WinZip
Web site:	http://www.winzip.com
Price:	US $29 (single-user licence)

System requirements:	• Windows 3.1/95/98/NT/2000/ME
Additional comments:	• Can be used for file compression/ decompression and encoding/decoding
Online reviews:	• http://www.pcquest.com/june00/ rev_winzip8.asp • http://www.simplythebest.net/gold/ winzip.html

B.4 Corpus-analysis software

Some questions to ask vendors when choosing corpus-analysis software to meet your needs:

- What languages and character sets are supported? Is the system double-byte enabled?
- What file formats are supported?
- Can multiple files be processed simultaneously?
- What types of searches are supported (e.g., wildcard, case-sensitive, context, bilingual query)?
- What display formats are used (e.g., KWIC, sentence, paragraph, full-text, side-by-side bilingual display)?
- What methods of sorting are supported?
- Does the tool support lemmatization and stop lists?
- What formula is used to generate collocates (e.g., mutual information scores)?
- What other tools or features are included (e.g., alignment tools for bilingual concordancers)?
- What are the system requirements (e.g., operating system, hardware)?
- What is the cost of the software/upgrades/technical support?
- Who are some of your current clients/users? Can I contact them to ask their opinion about your product?

Product name:	MonoConc Pro
Web site:	http://www.athel.com/mono.html
Price:	US $129 (single-user licence), US $85 (educational price)

System requirements:	• Windows 95 or higher
Additional comments:	• Monolingual concordancer
Online reviews:	• http://linguistlist.org/issues/11/11-1411.html • http://astro.temple.edu/~jburston/CALICO/review/monoconc.htm • http://llt.msu.edu/vol5num3/review4/default.html

Product name:	Multiconcord
Web site:	http://web.bham.ac.uk/johnstf/lingua.htm
Price:	UK £40
System requirements:	• Windows 3.x/95 • 4 MB RAM minimum
Additional comments:	• Bilingual concordancer • Comes with software to mark up texts for automatic alignment • Alignment is done "on the fly" and it takes place at sentence and paragraph level
Online reviews:	• http://www.hull.ac.uk/cti/pubs/newsletter/mar98.htm #MULTICONCORD • http://www.hull.ac.uk/cti/resources/reviews/multiconc.htm

Product name:	ParaConc
Web site:	http://www.ruf.rice.edu/~barlow/parac.html or http://www.athel.com
Price:	US $139 (single-user licence)
System requirements:	• Windows 95 or higher

Additional comments:	• Bilingual concordancer • Attempts to identify translation equivalents at word level • Allows search terms in source and target languages to be sorted independently
Online reviews:	• http://www.benjamins.com/jbp/journals/Ijcl/Ijcl_41.html#Barlow

Product name:	WordSmith Tools
Web site:	http://www.oup.com/elt/global/catalogue/multimedia/wordsmithtools3/
Price:	UK £51.95 (single-user licence)
System requirements:	• Windows 3.1x or Windows 95 • 80386 processor minimum • 4 MB RAM minimum (8 MB for Windows 95)
Additional comments:	• Primarily a monolingual concordancer with some alignment features • Includes word lister, concordancer, collocation viewer, and several other tools
Online reviews:	• http://www.cltr.uq.edu.au/oncall/wright111.html • http://info.ox.ac.uk/ctitext/publish/comtxt/ct12/sardinha.html • http://llt.msu.edu/vol5num3/review4/default.html

B.5 Terminology-management and translation-memory systems

Terminology-management and translation-memory systems are frequently integrated, and so they have been treated together in this section. The following are some questions to ask vendors when choosing terminology-management and translation-memory systems to meet your needs:

• Do these tools come as an integrated package or can they be purchased and operated as standalone components?

- What other tools are included as part of an integrated package (e.g., alignment tool, filters, term-extraction tool)?
- What additional tools can be integrated with this system (e.g., word processors, machine-translation systems)?
- What languages and character sets are supported? Is the system double-byte enabled?
- What file formats are supported? Are the TBX and TMX standards supported?
- Can existing glossaries and TM databases be imported?
- What are the units of segmentation?
- What types of matches are possible (e.g., exact, full, fuzzy, term, sub-segment)?
- Can the system be networked?
- What are the system requirements (e.g., operating system, hardware)?
- What is the cost of software/upgrades/training/technical support?
- Who are some of your current clients/users? Can I contact them to ask their opinion about your product?

Product name:	Déjà Vu
Web site:	http://www.atril.com
Price:	€ 990
System requirements:	• Windows 95/98/NT 4.0/2000 • Pentium II processor • 64MB RAM
Additional comments:	• Includes TermWatch terminology-management tool and an alignment tool • Free technical support
Online reviews: ,	• http://www.accurapid.com/journal/03TM1.htm • http://www.languagepartners.com/dvi/lingualizer.htm • http://www.star-ag.ch/press/tm-review01.htm • http://www.star-ag.ch/press/tm-review02.htm

Product name:	IBM Translation Manager
Web site:	http://www-4.ibm.com/software/ad/translat/tm/
Price:	US $2,149

System requirements:	• OS/2/Windows 95/98/NT • 386 processor or higher • 8 MB RAM • 100 MB hard disk
Additional comments:	• Includes alignment and terminology-management features
Online reviews:	• http://www.accurapid.com/journal/03TM2.htm • http://www.star-ag.ch/press/tm-review01.htm • http://www.star-ag.ch/press/tm-review02.htm

Product name:	MultiTrans
Web site:	http://www.multicorpora.ca/emultitrans.html
Price:	US $2,219 (Pro), US $689 (Lite)
System requirements:	• Windows 95/98/NT • Microsoft Word 97/2000 for TransTerm module • Pentium 200 MHz • 32 MB RAM • 800 X 600 display • 20 MB free hard disk space
Additional comments:	• Includes TermBase terminology-management system and term-extraction tools • Does "on the fly" alignment • Uses sub-segment matching • Some specialized dictionaries available

Product name:	SDLX
Web site:	http://www.sdlintl.com/products/sdlx/nav/main.htm
Price:	US $595 (standard), US $1,195 (professional)

System requirements:	• Windows 95/98/2000/NT • Pentium 90 (Pentium 233 recommended) • 32 MB RAM minimum (64 MB recommended) • 20 MB free hard disk space
Additional comments:	• Includes SDL Termbase and SDL Align
Online reviews:	• http://www.star-ag.ch/press/tm-review01.htm • http://www.star-ag.ch/press/tm-review02.htm • http://www.sdlintl.com/products/sdlx/nav/main.htm • http://www.crux.be/English/IJLD/ijld_sdlxreview.pdf

Product name:	STAR TransIT Professional
Web site:	http://www.star-transit.com/en/
Price:	€ 1,245 (Satellite Personal Edition can be downloaded for free)
System requirements:	• Windows 95/98/2000/NT • Pentium 133 MHz • 32 MB RAM (Windows 95), 48 MB RAM (Windows 98/2000/NT) • 80 MB free hard disk space
Additional comments:	• Includes TermStar terminology-management system and alignment tool • Technical support is not free
Online reviews:	• http://www.accurapid.com/journal/03TM2.htm • http://www.star-ag.ch/press/tm-review01.htm • http://www.star-ag.ch/press/tm-review02.htm

Product name:	TRADOS 5
Web site:	http://www.trados.com
Price:	US $795 (Freelance edition)

System requirements:	• Windows 95/98/NT/ME • Pentium II or higher • 64 MB RAM minimum
Additional comments:	• Includes Multiterm terminology-management system and WinAlign alignment software • Monolingual and bilingual term-extraction tools also available • Can be integrated with Logos and Systran machine-translation systems
Online reviews:	• http://www.crux.be/English/IJLD/ IJLD_trados3review.pdf • http://www.accurapid.com/journal/ 03TM2.htm • http://www.star-ag.ch/press/tm-review01.htm • http://www.star-ag.ch/press/tm-review02.htm • http://www.trados.com/about/ testimonials.asp

B.6 Localization and Web-page translation tools

Some questions to ask vendors when choosing localization and Web-page translation tools to meet your needs:

- What file formats are supported?
- What languages and character sets are supported? Is the system double-byte enabled?
- What tools and features are included in the package (e.g., editors, validation, spell checking, leveraging, glossary support)?
- What are the system requirements (e.g., operating system, hardware)?
- What is the cost of the software/upgrades/technical support?
- Who are some of your current clients/users? Can I contact them to ask their opinion about your product?

Product name:	Alchemy CATALYST (formerly Corel CATALYST)
Web site:	http://www.alchemysoftware.ie/products/ catalyst4_0.html
Price:	US $599 (translator edition), US $3,499 (localizer edition)

System requirements:	• Windows 95/98/2000/NT • 16 MB RAM (32 MB recommended) • 20 MB free hard disk space
Additional comments:	• Includes editors, glossary support, project-management features, spell checking, leveraging, and validation functionality
Online reviews:	• http://www.languagepartners.com/catalyst/success-index.html

Product name:	PASSOLO
Web site:	http://www.passolo.com
Price:	€ 600 (programmer's edition), € 750 (professional edition)
System requirements:	• Windows 95/98/2000/NT • Intel Processor 80486/100 or Pentium • 32 MB RAM • 8 MB free hard disk space
Additional comments:	• For languages with special character sets a localized version of the operating system is needed • For Asian languages, Windows NT or Windows 2000 must be used to enable Unicode support • An interface for use with TRADOS tools is available
Online reviews:	• http://www.passolo.com/site/us/features/press.htm • http://www.crux.be/English/IJLD/IJLD8_passolo.pdf

Product name:	Trans Web Express
Web site:	http://www.berlitz.ie/twe
Price:	Freeware. There is no charge for the fully functional version.

System requirements:	• Windows95/NT • Netscape Navigator 3.01 or Microsoft Internet Explorer 3.02 or higher • 486 DX or higher • 16 MB RAM • 10 MB free hard disk space
Additional comments:	• For localizing HTML files
Online reviews:	• http://www.berlitz.ie/twe/li_review.html

B.7 Word-counting tools

Some questions to ask vendors when choosing word-counting tools to meet your needs:

- What file formats are supported?
- What are the system requirements (e.g., operating system, hardware)?
- What is the cost of software/upgrades/technical support?
- Who are some of your current clients/users? Can I contact them to ask their opinion about your product?

Product name:	Free Budget
Web site:	http://www.webbudget.com/freebudget/features.htm
Price:	Freeware. There is no charge for the fully functional version.
System requirements:	• Windows 95/98/2000/NT • MS Word 97 (or higher) • Pentium processor • 16 MB RAM • 2 MB free disk space
Additional comments:	• Includes 6 months of free updates and 6 months of technical support by e-mail • Supports Rich Text Format (.rtf), Word (.doc) and text (.txt) files

| Online reviews: | • http://office.tucows.com/preview/60482.html
• http://www.zdnet.com/downloads/stories/
info/0,,001C5G,.html |

Product name:	PDFCount for Acrobat
Web site:	http://www.pdfcount.com/
Price:	US $59.95 (single-user license)
System requirements:	• Windows 95/98/NT
Additional comments:	• Supports Adobe Acrobat Reader 3.01 (or higher), Acrobat Exchange 3.01 or Acrobat 4.0 • Does not support text imbedded in graphics or PDF files created with Subset True Type Fonts.
Online reviews:	• http://denver.bcentral.com/denver/stories/2000/01/24/story8.html

Product name:	Web Budget
Web site:	http://www.webbudget.com
Price:	US $89 (free demo version available)
System requirements:	• Windows 95/98/2000/NT • Pentium processor • 16 MB RAM • 2 MB free disk space
Additional comments:	• Includes 6 months of free updates and 6 months of technical support by e-mail • Supports HTML and text files
Online reviews:	• http://www.zdnet.com/pcmag/stories/trends/0,7607,2340059,00.html

B.8 Cost/benefit estimators

Some questions to ask vendors when choosing a cost/benefit estimator to meet your needs:

- For which types of tools or products does this tool produce cost/benefit estimates?
- What are the system requirements (e.g., operating system, hardware)?
- What is the cost of the software/upgrades/technical support?
- Who are some of your current clients/users? Can I contact them to ask their opinion about your product?

Product name:	CBE Cost Benefit Estimator
Web site:	http://www.languagepartners.com/downloads/cbe/index.html
Price:	Freeware. There is no charge for the fully functional version.
System requirements:	• Excel/MS-Office 95 or 97
Additional comments:	• Provides a first-cut estimate of the costs and benefits associated with using CAT tools • Price schedules for the following tools are included: Déjà Vu, Star TransIT, TRADOS • Users can modify/add to the schedules to reflect price changes or other products of interest

References

Ahmad, Khurshid, and Margaret Rogers. 2001. "Corpus Linguistics and Terminology Extraction." In Sue Ellen Wright and Gerhard Budin (eds.), *Handbook of Terminology Management* , vol. 2, 725–60. Amsterdam and Philadelphia: John Benjamins.

Ahrenberg, Lars, and Magnus Merkel. 1996. "On Translation Corpora and Translation Support Tools: A Project Report." In Karin Aijmer, Bengt Altenberg, and Mats Johansson (eds.), *Languages in Contrast*, 183–200. Lund: Lund University Press.

Andrés Lange, Carmen, and Winfield Scott Bennett. 2000. "Combining Machine Translation with Translation Memory at Baan." In Robert C. Sprung (ed.), *Translating into Success: Cutting-Edge Strategies for Going Multilingual in a Global Age*, 201–18. Amsterdam and Philadelphia: John Benjamins.

Arnold, Doug, Lorna Balkan, R. Lee Humphreys, Siety Meijer, and Louisa Sadler. 1994. *Machine Translation: An Introductory Guide*. Oxford: NCC and Oxford Blackwell.

Austermühl, Frank. 2001. *Electronic Tools for Translators*. Manchester: St. Jerome Publishing.

Baker, Mona. 1992. *In Other Words: A Coursebook on Translation*. London: Routledge.

– 1996. "Corpus-Based Translation Studies: The Challenges that Lie Ahead." In Harold L. Somers (ed.), *Terminology, LSP and Translation: Studies in Language Engineering in Honour of Juan C. Sager*, 175–86. Amsterdam and Philadelphia: John Benjamins.

Barnbrook, Geoff. 1996. *Language and Computers*. Edinburgh: Edinburgh University Press.

Bédard, Claude. 1998. "Ce qu'il faut savoir sur les mémoires de traduction." *Circuit*, 60: 25–26.

Belaïd, Abdel. 1998. "OCR: Print." In Giovanni Varile and Antonio Zampolli (eds.), *Survey of the State of the Art in Human Language Technology*, 71–74. Cambridge: Cambridge University Press.

Bennison, Peter, and Lynne Bowker. 2000. "Designing a Tool for Exploiting Bilingual Comparable Corpora." In Maria Gavrilidou, George Carayannis, Stella Markantonatou, Stelios Piperidas, and Gregory Stainhaouer (eds.), *Proceedings of the 2nd International Conference on Language Resources and Evaluation)*, vol. 1, 513–16. Paris: ELRA.

Bergeron, Manon, and Susan Larsson. 1999. "Internet Search Strategies for Translators." *ATA Chronicle*, 28 (7): 22–25.

Bouillon, Pierrette, and André Clas, eds. 1993. *La Traductique*. Montreal: Les Presses de l'Université de Montréal.

Bowker, Lynne. 1996. "Towards a Corpus-Based Approach to Terminography." *Terminology*, 3 (1): 27–52.

– 1998. "Using Specialized Monolingual Native Language Corpora as a Translation Resource: A Pilot Study." *Meta*, 43 (4): 631–51.

– 2000. "Towards a Methodology for Exploiting Specialized Target Language Corpora as Translation Resources." *International Journal of Corpus Linguistics* 5 (1): 17–52.

Bowker, Lynne, and Jennifer Pearson. 2002. *Working with Specialized Language: A Practical Guide to Using Corpora*. London: Routledge.

Brooks, David. 2000. "What Price Globalization? Managing Costs at Microsoft." In Robert C. Sprung (ed.), *Translating into Success: Cutting-Edge Strategies for Going Multilingual in a Global Age*, 43–57. Amsterdam and Philadelphia: John Benjamins.

Cabré, M. Teresa, Rosa Estopà, and Jordi Vivaldi. 2001. "Automatic Term Detection: A Review of Current Systems." In Didier Bourigault, Christian Jacquemin, and Marie-Claude L'Homme (eds.), *Recent Advances in Computational Terminology*, 53-87. Amsterdam and Philadelphia: John Benjamins.

Cheng, Susan. 2000. "Globalizing an e-Commerce Web Site." In Robert C. Sprung (ed.), *Translating into Success: Cutting-Edge Strategies for Going Multilingual in a Global Age*, 29–42. Amsterdam and Philadelphia: John Benjamins.

Clark, Robert. 1994. "Computer-Assisted Translation: The State of the Art." In Cay Dollerup and Annette Lindegaard (eds.), *Teaching Translation and Interpreting 2: Insights, Aims, Visions*, 301–08. Amsterdam and Philadelphia: John Benjamins.

Cleary, Róisín, and Reinhard Schäler. 2000. "R&D Opens Doors to Translation Portals." *Localisation Ireland*, 4 (1): 9.

Corbolante, Licia, and Ulrike Irmler. 2001. "Software Terminology and Localization." In Sue Ellen Wright and Gerhard Budin (eds.), *Handbook of Terminology Management*, vol. 2, 516–35. Amsterdam and Philadelphia: John Benjamins.

DeCesaris, Janet Ann. 1996. "Computerized Translation Managers as Teaching Aids." In Cay Dollerup and Vibeke Appel (eds.), *Teaching Translation and Interpreting 3: New Horizons*, 263–69. Amsterdam and Philadelphia: John Benjamins.

De Schaetzen, Caroline. 1997. "L'enseignement de la terminotique: spécificités et contraintes." *Terminologies nouvelles*, 17: 14–26.

Dubuc, Robert. 1985. *Manuel pratique de terminologie*. 2d ed. Montreal: Linguatech.

Ebeling, Jarle. 1998. "Contrastive Linguistics, Translation, and Parallel Corpora." *Meta*, 43 (4): 602–15.

Engwall, Gunnel. 1994. "Not Chance but Choice: Criteria in Corpus Creation." In Sue Atkins and Antonio Zampolli (eds.), *Computational Approaches to the Lexicon*, 49–82. Oxford: Oxford University Press.

Esselink, Bert. 2000. *A Practical Guide to Localization*. Rev. ed. Amsterdam and Philadelphia: John Benjamins.

Fry, Deborah. 2000. *The Localization Industry Primer*. Féchy, Switzerland: Localization Industry Standards Association (LISA).

Garside, Roger, Geoffrey Leech, and Tony McEnery, eds. 1997. *Corpus Annotation: Linguistic Information from Computer Text Corpora*. London: Longman.

Gaussier, Eric. 2001. "General considerations on bilingual terminology extraction." In Didier Bourigault, Christian Jacquemin, and Marie-Claude L'Homme (eds.), *Recent Advances in Computational Terminology*, 167-183. Amsterdam and Philadelphia: John Benjamins.

Gouadec, Daniel. 1994. "Traduction et Informatique: les implications pour la formation." *Langages*, 116: 59–74.

Hatim, Basil, and Ian Mason. 1990. *Discourse and the Translator*. London: Longman.

Haynes, Colin. 1998. *Breaking Down the Language Barriers*. London: Aslib.

Heyn, Mattias. 1998. "Translation Memories: Insights and Prospects." In Lynne Bowker, Michael Cronin, Dorothy Kenny, and Jennifer Pearson (eds.), *Unity in Diversity? Current Trends in Translation Studies*, 123–36. Manchester: St. Jerome Publishing.

Hofmann, Cornelia, and Thorsten Mehnert. "Multilingual Information Management at Schneider Automation." In Robert C. Sprung (ed.), *Translating into Success: Cutting-Edge Strategies for Going Multilingual in a Global Age*, 60–79. Amsterdam and Philadelphia: John Benjamins.

Holmes, James S. 1988. *Translated! Papers on Literary Translation and Translation Studies*. Amsterdam: Rodopi.

Hutchins, W. John, and Harold L. Somers. 1992. *An Introduction to Machine Translation*. London: Academic Press.

Isabelle, Pierre. 1993. "Bi-textual Aids for Translators." Technical Report. Laval, Quebec: Centre for Information Technologies Innovation.

Jaekel, Gary. 2000. "Terminology Management at Ericsson." In Robert C. Sprung (ed.), *Translating into Success: Cutting-Edge Strategies for Going Multilingual in a Global Age*, 159–71. Amsterdam and Philadelphia: John Benjamins.

Kageura, Kyo, and Bin Umino. 1996. "Methods of Automatic Term Recognition: A Review." *Terminology*, 3 (2): 259–90.

Kay, Martin, and Martin Röscheisen. 1993. "Text Translation Alignment." *Computational Linguistics*, 19 (1): 121–42.

Kennedy, Graeme. 1998. *An Introduction to Corpus Linguistics*. London: Longman.

Kenny, Dorothy. 1999. "CAT Tools in an Academic Environment: What Are They Good For?" *Target*, 11 (1): 65–82.

Kingscott, Geoffrey. 1996. "The Impact of Technology and the Implications for Teaching." In Cay Dollerup and Vibeke Appel (eds.), *Teaching Translation and Interpreting 3: New Horizons*, 295–300. Amsterdam and Philadelphia: John Benjamins.

Kohlmeier, Bernhard. 2000. "Microsoft Encarta goes Multilingual." In Robert C. Sprung (ed.), *Translating into Success: Cutting-Edge Strategies for Going Multilingual in a Global Age*, 1–11. Amsterdam and Philadelphia: John Benjamins.

Lauriston, Andy. 1997. "Terminology and the Computer." In Robert Dubuc, *Terminology: A Practical Approach* (trans. Elaine Kennedy), 179-192. Brossard, Québec: Linguatech.

Laviosa, Sara. 1998. "The English Comparable Corpus: A Resource and a Methodology." In Lynne Bowker, Michael Cronin, Dorothy Kenny, and Jennifer Pearson (eds.), *Unity in Diversity? Current Trends in Translation Studies*, 101–12. Manchester: St. Jerome Publishing.

L'Homme, Marie-Claude. 1999a. *Initiation à la traductique*. Brossard, Quebec: Linguatech.

– 1999b. "Apports et limites de l'informatique." In Daniel Gouadec (ed.), *Formation des traducteurs*, 109–21. Paris: La Maison du Dictionnaire.

Lindquist, Hans. 1999. "Electronic Corpora as Tools for Translation." In Gunilla Anderman and Margaret Rogers (eds.), *Words, Text, Translation: Liber Amicorum for Peter Newmark*, 179–89. Clevedon: Multilingual Matters.

Lockwood, Rose. 2000. "Machine Translation and Controlled Authoring at Caterpillar." In Robert C. Sprung (ed.), *Translating into Success: Cutting-Edge Strategies for Going Multilingual in a Global Age*, 187–202. Amsterdam and Philadelphia: John Benjamins.

Loffler-Laurian, Anne-Marie. 1996. *La traduction automatique*. Villeneuve d'Ascq, France: Presses universitaires du Septentrion.

Macklovitch, Elliott and Graham Russell. 2000. "What's Been Forgotten in Translation Memory." In John White (ed.), *Envisioning Machine Translation in the Information Future: Proceedings of AMTA 2000*, 137–46. Berlin: Springer Verlag.

Macklovitch, Elliott, Michel Simard, and Philippe Langlais. 2000. "TransSearch: A Free Translation Memory on the World Wide Web." In Maria Gavrilidou, George Carayannis, Stella Markantonatou, Stelios Piperidas, and Gregory Stainhaouer (eds.), *Proceedings of the 2nd International Conference on Language Resources and Evaluation*, vol. 3, 1201–08. Paris: ELRA.

Maia, Belinda. 1998. "Word Order and the First Person Singular in Portuguese and English." *Meta*, 43 (4): 589–601.

McEnery, Tony, and Andrew Wilson. 1996. *Corpus Linguistics*. Edinburgh: Edinburgh University Press.

Melby, Alan. 1998. "Behind the Scenes: Data-Exchange Standards are Unsung Heroes Revolutionizing the Language Industries." *Language International*, 10 (6): 30–31.

Melby, Alan, Klaus-Dirk Schmitz, and Sue Ellen Wright. 2001. "Terminology Interchange." In Sue Ellen Wright and Gerhard Budin (eds.), *Handbook of Terminology Management*, vol. 2, 613–42. Amsterdam and Philadelphia: John Benjamins.

Melby, Alan K., with Terry C. Warner. 1995. *The Possibility of Language: A Discussion of the Nature of Language with Implications for Human and Machine Translation*. Amsterdam and Philadelphia: John Benjamins.

Meyer, Ingrid, and Kristen Mackintosh. 1996. "The Corpus from a Terminographer's Viewpoint." *International Journal of Corpus Linguistics*, 1 (2): 257–85.

Norton, Peter, and John Goodman. 1997. *Peter Norton's Inside the PC*. 7th ed. Indianapolis: Sams Publishing.

O'Brien, Sharon. 1998. "Practical Experience of Computer-Aided Translation Tools in the Localization Industry." In Lynne Bowker, Michael Cronin, Dorothy Kenny, and Jennifer Pearson (eds.), *Unity in Diversity? Current Trends in Translation Studies*, 115–22. Manchester: St. Jerome Publishing.

Otman, Gabriel. 1991. "Aspects de l'informatisation des activités terminologiques et traductionnelles." *Terminologies nouvelles*, 5: 15–20.

Pearson, Jennifer. 1996. "Electronic Text and Concordances in the Translation Classroom." *Teanga*, 16: 85–95.

– 1998. *Terms in Context*. Amsterdam and Philadelphia: John Benjamins.

Rayner, Manny, David Carter, Pierrette Bouillon, Vassilis Digalakis, and Mats Wirén, eds. 2000. *The Spoken Language Translator*. Cambridge: Cambridge University Press.

Rode, Tony. 2000, April. "Translation Memory: Friend or Foe?" *International Journal for Language and Documentation*, 12–13.

Rondeau, Guy. 1984. *Introduction à la terminologie*. 2d ed. Boucherville: Gaëtan Morin.

Roumen, Rob, and Theo van der Ster. "Context: A New Concept in Computer-Aided Translation." In Klaus-Dirk Schmitz (ed.), *TKE'93: Terminology and Knowledge Engineering*, 215–20. Frankfurt: Indeks-Verlag.

Sager, Juan C. 1990. *A Practical Course in Terminology Processing*. Amsterdam and Philadelphia: John Benjamins.

– 1994. *Language Engineering and Translation: Consequences of Automation*. Amsterdam and Philadelphia: John Benjamins.

Samuelsson-Brown, Geoffrey. 1996. "New Technology for Translators." In Rachel Owens (ed.), *The Translator's Handbook*, 3d ed., 279–93. London: Aslib.

Schäler, Reinhard. 1998. "The Problem with Machine Translation." In Lynne Bowker, Michael Cronin, Dorothy Kenny and Jennifer Pearson (eds.), *Unity in Diversity? Current Trends in Translation Studies*, 151–56. Manchester: St. Jerome Publishing.

Scherf, Willi G. 1992. "Training, Talent and Technology." In Cay Dollerup and Anne Loddegaard (ed.), *Teaching Translation and Interpreting: Training, Talent and Experience*, 153–160. Amsterdam and Philadelphia: John Benjamins.

Schmitz, Klaus-Dirk, 1996. "Terminology Management Systems." In Rachel Owens (ed.), *The Translator's Handbook*, 3d ed , 221–39. London: Aslib.

– 2001. "Criteria for Evaluating Terminology Database Management Programs." In Sue Ellen Wright and Gerhard Budin (eds.), *Handbook of Terminology Management*, vol. 2, 539–51. Amsterdam and Philadelphia: John Benjamins.

Sprung, Robert C. 2000. "Introduction." In Robert C. Sprung (ed.), *Translating into Success: Cutting-Edge Strategies for Going Multilingual in a Global Age*, ix–xxii. Amsterdam and Philadelphia: John Benjamins.

Sprung, Robert C., and Alberto Vourvoulias-Bush. 2000. "Adapting Time Magazine for Latin America." In Robert C. Sprung (ed.), *Translating into Success: Cutting-Edge Strategies for Going Multilingual in a Global Age*, 13–27. Amsterdam and Philadelphia: John Benjamins.

Thibodeau, Ricky P. 2000. "Making a Global Product at MapInfo Corporation." In Robert C. Sprung (ed.), *Translating into Success: Cutting-Edge Strategies for Going Multilingual in a Global Age*, 127–46. Amsterdam and Philadelphia: John Benjamins.

Topping, Suzanne. 2000a. "Shortening the Translation Cycle at Eastman Kodak." In Robert C. Sprung (ed.), *Translating into Success: Cutting-Edge Strategies for Going Multilingual in a Global Age*, 111–25. Amsterdam and Philadelphia: John Benjamins.

– 2000b. "Sharing Translation Database Information: Considerations for developing an ethical and viable exchange of data." *Multilingual Computing and Technology*, 11 (5): 59–61.

Toury, Gideon. 1980. *In Search of a Theory of Translation*. Tel Aviv: Porter Institute for Poetics and Semiotics.

Trujillo, Arturo. 1999. *Translation Engines: Techniques for Machine Translation*. London: Springer-Verlag.

Unicode Consortium, eds. 2000. *The Unicode Standard Version 3.0*. Reading, MA: Addison-Wesley Publishing Co.

Wahlster, Wolfgang, ed. 2000. *Verbmobil: Foundations of Speech-to-Speech Translation*. Berlin: Springer-Verlag.

Wältermann, Dieter. 1994. "Machine Translation Systems in a Translation Curriculum." In Cay Dollerup and Annette Lindegaard (eds.), *Teaching Translation and Interpreting 2: Insights, Aims, Visions*, 309–17. Amsterdam and Philadelphia: John Benjamins.

Warburton, Kara. 2001. "Globalization and Terminology Management." In Sue Ellen Wright and Gerhard Budin (eds.), *Handbook of Terminology Management*, vol. 2, 677–96. Amsterdam and Philadelphia: John Benjamins.

Webb, Lynn E. 1998. *Advantages and Disadvantages of Translation Memory: A Cost/Benefit Analysis*. MA Thesis, Monterey Institute of International Studies, California.

Wright, Sue Ellen. 2001. "Terminology Management Entry Structures." In Sue Ellen Wright and Gerhard Budin (eds.), *Handbook of Terminology Management*, vol. 2, 572–99. Amsterdam and Philadelphia: John Benjamins.

Zanettin, Federico. 1998. "Bilingual Comparable Corpora and the Training of Translators." *Meta*, 43 (4): 616–30.

Index